Copyright © 2022 Karen.B.Martushev.

All rights reserved. No part of this book may be used or reproduced by any means, graphic, electronic, or mechanical, including photocopying, recording, taping or by any information storage retrieval system without the written permission of the author except in the case of brief quotations embodied in critical articles and reviews.

Balboa Press books may be ordered through booksellers or by contacting:

Balboa Press
A Division of Hay House
1663 Liberty Drive
Bloomington, IN 47403
www.balboapress.com
844-682-1282

Because of the dynamic nature of the Internet, any web addresses or links contained in this book may have changed since publication and may no longer be valid. The views expressed in this work are solely those of the author and do not necessarily reflect the views of the publisher, and the publisher hereby disclaims any responsibility for them.

Cover design by Nitika Tiwari

Print information available on the last page.

ISBN: 978-1-9822-7830-4 (sc)
ISBN: 978-1-9822-7832-8 (hc)
ISBN: 978-1-9822-7831-1 (e)

Library of Congress Control Number: 2021924941

Balboa Press rev. date: 12/21/2021

OWN YOUR DARKNESS

BECOME THE PROPRIETOR OF YOUR OWN DARKNESS &
TRANSFORM IT INTO YOUR GREATEST ASSET.

KAREN.B.MARTUSHEV

BALBOA.PRESS
A DIVISION OF HAY HOUSE

I dedicate this book to all those who are on a journey inward, who seek to master their pain, and those who were planted in a circumstance of pain to grow into their own deep soul purpose: the higher self of existence, the awakened. Outgrowing the pain and growing into bliss where pain can't thrive is our true nature and who we truly are.

If you are seeking self-help in dark times in your life as I did, I hope this book will bring you understanding like it did for me when I wrote it. I hope it leaves you with the understanding to rise into your divine purpose and undertake a beautiful direction in your life. Those who found this book to read, yet could not receive the guidance and answers that they were hoping for, I hope it still brings resolution in some way and aligns you with your destined path.

—— Karen

CONTENTS

A Note to the Reader xi
Introduction xiii
Preface xxi

Chapter 1   Emotions 1
Chapter 2   Emerging Into True Myself 9
Chapter 3   Depression 21
Chapter 4   Solitude 33
Chapter 5   Sadness 43
Chapter 6   Criticism 51
Chapter 7   Frustration 61
Chapter 8   Self-doubt 71
Chapter 9   Self-Forgiveness 81
Chapter 10 Self Hate 89
Chapter 11 Ego 97
Chapter 12 The snob in us 107
Chapter 13 We Judge 115
Chapter 14 Neglect 123
Chapter 15 Bliss 131
Chapter 16 Self-Rebirth 139

A NOTE TO THE READER

Karen is aware she's not alone in writing this book. More than half of this book was dialoged to her by spirit guides from divine realms, archangels, and those of a consciousness (as an energies of divine beings or in service of helping humanity and share wisdom) her highest self, and those who have died and didn't go to gods' lands (ghosts). These guides desire to help in some way, whether to share wisdom or teach mastery of some kind.

Karen's words and those from her highest self will be formatted like this: unitalicized. The wisdom from spiritual masters, divine channels, and spirit guides will be in italics and often use the pronoun "we" or say Karen's name verses saying "I" so you'll always know where the wisdom you're reading is coming from.

We have gathered to assist Karen to write this book so that it will be available to those who are seeking. It is a team effort. Karen and all of us are all here helping this book to become.

Certain things she shares are her intimate moments with the spirit. Those realms that are unusual and spoken less often about are called "darkness." For darkness is not what it seems to be to the outside world. We all have darkness within us that we must cultivate and become, work in tandem with instead of wrestling with, in order to understand ourselves and the unique darkness in each of us resides.

Karen is gifted and knowledgeable about certain things not all human consciousness is ready to receive and it is that understanding of things she carries within her that allowed this book to be written. As she carries the wisdom, we are here to confirm that it is true, for the knowledge was given to her through realms of spiritual guidance and divine consciousness. She is highly attuned and is able to receive messages from the divine and realms of the spirit. She was young and understood energy beyond words but has worked to convey that energy in words in this book. She is a crystal child and the energies of crystals are the homes of the divine.

Each child is born with a unique aura color and purpose instilled. As for Karen, she rules the crown chakra, as her aura is lavender and her purpose lies there as a spiritual teacher, guide, and divine channel. We all can look within ourselves and will find our home and discover where we all came from. For this inner path towards self is a dedication for those who have been asked to evolve and assist humanity in one way or another.

INTRODUCTION

At this moment if you are sitting and thinking to yourself, as I did, "If I could better my life or rise above what is going on within myself and within my mind, what would my life look like then? Who would I *be* then?" The question then seeped in: "Why do I live like this? Why me?" I was hoping the answers would come sooner, but instead something else took its place.

The beginning

The restrictions that were in my life from day one were that I was born into a Russian Old Believer religion. When I look back today, no matter how restrictive the religion was, it truly molded me to be who I am today with a deep purpose instilled in me that was waiting to be unraveled. It also instilled a deep understanding of certain things that I wouldn't understand otherwise, as well as a deeper, more serious approach to life. The freedom of full self-expression was restricted and other things took its place instead, such as being prepared in one way or another. Or as I like to think in my case, this included being exposed to spirituality more than a normal human being, eating for soul purposes, praying, spiritually disciplined daily practices, detaching from certain foods when required due to the religion, understanding how to read Russian and Slavanic languages, etc. The church of Russian religion and its way of living took place in much of my youth and into my late twenties. The obligations included traditional wear, which was very beautiful, very glamorous, and very high fashion due to the Russian high level standards, especially on big holidays and great events such as weddings. Although the traditional clothes were worn every day, not just a day or two days of the week, all clothes were custom made, custom designed, and could not be found in a regular store. The clothes were truly celebratory and were always admired when going out into public where not much of this apparel was worn by the general public. The culture overall was very rich but also very traditional. The women were not allowed to wear pants or show their hair after marriage. Married women covered their hair with stunning silk chiffon scarves with beaded ends or tassels. I wore these scarves as well, covering my hair for 16 years, before I went into my spiritual solo path. As I did, all the fancy, luxurious scarves I accumulated over the 16 years I gave away, only leaving one or two for myself to honor my roots and where I came from.

The food diet and tradition was designed based on a yearly plan taken from the Bible. The rules included how and when to eat fish and on what days, only kippered, or fully raw that can be cooked, or only caviar. There were the oil days only, meaning no meat or dairy that day or week, and there were days where no oil was given, so more fresh produce consumption took place. There were great recipes for vegan days, oil days, and fish days, and some people in the culture would be really creative and make the most delicious foods, at times tasting like it's not vegan at all. This would be practiced throughout the whole community, and those who would break this food diet would be talked about for how sinful it was, for this diet was looked upon as a very sacred way to cleanse the soul.

Although, at times I looked forward to these activities for it was during this time I used to detox, lose toxic body fats, staying away from alcohol drinks, and instead practice juicing fruits and veggies. It was a great time to be super creative in cultivating yummy new vegan recipes, and bake dairy free breads of all kinds. It was easy to be healthy in the kitchen. Many of my cooking skills I accumulated during that time of exposure to the food diet and are still what I use till today.

The church and communal praying was very stern, controlled by the elders, and took place every weekend. Personal prayers took place each morning and evening. The culture believed in this saying—and I will share this with you, for I know how precious life is myself. "Pray and prepare yourself through soul cleansing each morning and night, for you never know when your life ends, but when it ends, you know your soul was cleansed for that night or day of the happening."

The relationships were expected to be within the traditional format, and to be kept within the community, including for friendships, marriages, and such. When I was growing up, the community was more based on stern traditional roles for men and women that really shifted into more modern times the past twenty years, giving much more leisure and freedom to practice self-care and self-providing, especially for the women in the culture. In my upbringing, as to what a woman's role was and what was expected of us was to be more at home, be a homemaker, seamstress, a cook, run the household and make sure all is in order. The male role was to provide financially, to lead, to provide a good home, to make sure all is in order in life, contribute to community events, and whatever else is needed.

Being in this religion really molded me to have high spiritual exposure. Going to Bible school six days a week from age 5 till 13, learning Slavanic, learning about and understanding the saints, their roles, their spiritual gifts and miracles they would practice here on earth... I can go on, but the bottom line is that religion really advanced me into my purpose and awakened me younger in life into high levels of spiritual metaphysical work.

When it was time for me to go on my own spiritual path, my spiritual gifts of energy work and much more of that part of myself opened up. This was not supported or well received by the religion. That was a time I always wondered why the hard life of awakening shows up for us to live through. I felt at times that it could have been easier, or there could have been more emotional support from family and friends, but there wasn't much given at the stage of awakening. Through this, I really didn't know what truly was really happening within myself. I was trying to make sense of it all.

I know not everyone needs to fulfill their soul purpose or awaken, but as I hit my mid-twenties, my life began to transform into something I never thought would be. The pain of judgements in the community arose in me, activating the eyes and mind to be more observant to how the culture approached certain things. At times all I could hear was chatter of "what she is doing, what is she wearing, what is she eating." This somehow awakened me beyond the ego to where, even though you don't wear, eat, or do as others want you to, you are still you. The ego was eating, doing, wearing, and the ego was what was being criticized.

Over the years things slowly began taking a turn within myself, and I began to feel more suffocated, which was not normal—or so I thought. I began to seek professional help and help from those who understood energy work. As I became more aligned with my freedom after working with a lovely Energy Facilitator for years, I was able to understand how easy energy work was for me and how it came naturally. I then began to discover and find what was seeking me, as there was no coincidence in why one would awaken randomly in their life to spiritual evolution and take the spiritual path—especially after being born into a religion. Over the next several years I took on a spiritual path to understand what truly was happening to me and what to do about it, which was unfolding in front of me. The pain then began. So much pain arose, which was not just in the body, but in my mind, relationships, work, everywhere. All was changing at once, not just one life sector at a time. For this, I asked… Why me?

When this happens, find ways to be more present in your life. Do things that make you present in the moment, like appreciation meditation near moving waters, listening to wilderness, immersing yourself in Hallmark movies, drinking dark warm red wine with your favorite chocolate, planting your favorite plants, singing songs that bring good memories, etc. Do things that bring warmth into your heart and as warmth arrives in the heart, the senses will activate and signal the face to smile again.

To be present with life is to live in the moment and be with you, your own self. It's your self-connecting with your inner divine. What drains your energy will take away the rest as well, including joy, peace, and fulfillment.

What is draining you today will drain you tomorrow. To detach from the drainage, you must become present with yourself. Find yourself and give to yourself. If needed, detach and be in solitude with your endeavors, your goals, your own craft that come from your deep heart of who you truly are, as a divine expression. Through such deep, heartfelt endeavors, we can become present with ourselves, our life, and take action from that place without depletion. When we're fulfilling our soul's needs, we can approach everything, both times of challenge and times of celebration, with strength of heart and deep knowing that it all has a destiny. You have a destiny too.

The evolutionary path is part of the darkness, which plays a great part in the birth of new consciousness that will raise evolution and a higher self in all of us. For darkness creates this birth, and through darkness new life emerges. This is why this book was granted to Karen to write and is meant to be shared. It is no coincidence that today of all days she is hearing these dialogs of higher self from the spirit guides, inner spirit, and the spirits of others around her—for she is rising from her darkness and is emerging in the new life that she has birthed through her raised consciousness.

The life of this new self was destiny, regardless of the professional help Karen sought or otherwise, that assisted with healing in the process of spiritual awakening, life transformations, shamanism, astral work, past and future regression work.

Pain

Sometimes we think pain is the root of all evil, yet it is only a messenger. Pain is intentionally there, at times to indicate something is off, or to grow and mold into more than what resides in us at this moment, and may come in many forms. Pain is one of the most powerful vehicles one can ever get into and not have a boring journey to the destination where the bloom of bliss takes place.

As emotional human beings, we yearn to feel good and to feel loved and have a sense of belonging, but sometimes we are intentionally planted into a circumstance, a location, or a relationship where we are to intentionally grow and evolve, rise for our destined purpose, and become masters of our emotion, existence, and our true creations. Through this, we can access our deepest existence of emotions and highest potential of our own internal and external self.

Spiritual pain shows up to bring humans more into themselves, into their deep hearts to sit in that deep knowing and remembrance of who they truly are, and being the master of their own heart.

To take the spiritual journey inward, pain will often be amplified in a way that it can awaken us to taking action; to be clear on something, or even to begin our evolutionary path. When it is time to do so, the pain will be to such an extent that one feels as if they are dying physically and emotionally. But it is not the heart that is dying, it is the ego, which is keeping the doors into the heart closed. As ego becomes the enemy, the heart opens inward and you begin to come into it, to master all the lessons you have come to receive and rise above. This is the way to rule your quest and find your soul purpose from the highest self of existence. One does not only rule the physical, but the spiritual aspect of themselves too.

As the question arises, "Why is pain so powerful?" the answer shows up to match. Because it allows two worlds to create the highest energy known to man: wisdom.

Wisdom is accumulation of lessons, thoughts, and emotions molded and blended into something only one from within can create through their highest self. This is how we share the beauty, the cultivation of mastery, and the divinity of mastering pain that truly births worlds, new beginnings, and beauty as liberation.

PREFACE

Into The Darkness

When we own our darkness so deep within us and become the seat of it, in that time, nothing can sit in or be it for us there, except our own divine, the true source of our own self. We conquer through that darkness our full embodiment of light from that place—for we know what the opposite of it is. As love is in all dimensions, it may be in our darkness as well in the most subtle ways. It may appear in the most profound ways, which cannot be shown when we are in our light.

Darkness occurs in one's life and may come to help to remember and obtain self power to become the light they came here to be, the authentic light they were given before incarnating here on earth. To some it may take a long time to remember, and awaken to, for others not so long because some are born naturally to remember it. Some need to step into it, to welcome the light in and become it. Before that, there are lessons and journeys to embody before one can truly stand in their own darkness yet be the light within themselves, and honor the light that was there all along.

Many don't know what really can or does go on behind the painful emotions and physical pain in the beginning of waking up to our remembrance and why in that phase it can take us so low emotionally within ourselves.

How do we actually get out of painful emotions, when we are being planted into them, to evolve, to understand something within us or awaken? And why do they occur?

That was my question when I hit the lowest, darkest part of myself, when my life changes came for me to step into and through to my light destination. This took more effect on me in the midst of moving house and being in the midst of my spiritual dark night of the soul. All this felt like it was going on forever, but it was actually a few years. In that time, depression was deeply felt and experienced on a very high level. But then I wondered, was it depression or much more and deeper than that?

The deepest dark place in me took residency when nothing made sense in the physical world. After leaving most of the family, community, tradition, religion and moving into the city, losing so much at once, or so it felt like, my heart went empty and felt empty for a long time. The pain then settled in, and this began the transmutational process for the new phase of life. Embodying so much change internally, activating spiritual gifts that were beyond my control at that time, I felt angry, even furious, and out of control. For this I sensed myself giving up and going inward into myself, into my dark place of myself, for nothing was waiting for me in the physical world––or so it felt that way.

The question yet lingered: What is deeper than depression, really?

I learned soon enough.

It was a place beyond what one could imagine, yet experienced. Yet again, how do we get out of what we truly don't understand?

How do we go about it so that we might come to understand and rise above it?

After years of being in my dark night of the soul transition, in the midst of it all, one day I just had enough. I dragged my feet on the carpeted floor, walking slowly in circles in my bedroom, feeling like I was hungover, with my mouth dry and my head heavy and throbbing. I didn't drink alcohol the night before, but the pain in my crown chakra was so excruciating that no Advil could help. I took out my mint green journal where I usually put all my thoughts to process through so that I might address them in order to find release, or to rise above.

In this case, I didn't realize that what I would write in that journal would become a book. Which I know may have some misspellings from time to time, sentences not structured to perfection, and that is ok, my importance was to share with you what was given.

My hand took the pen and began to write, but as I did, I could barely keep up. What went through me was a surge of high level energy and speed.

Throughout the next couple of days, which turned into months, and then a year plus, I wrote and collected what was given as dialogues, stories, memories, guidance, and self help. I would ask more questions about emotions from my spirit guides, seeking their wisdom, and those who were helping me understand, to remember, and to go through the darkness back to my authentic light.

My first question I wrote to ask myself to assess and get clear about was: "Why was the suffering recurrent? And why does this throbbing physical pain in my head and body exist with these negative emotions that keep showing up over and over again?"

Prior to my life transition, I studied the Law of Attraction, emotions, and high vibe living, and taught this information to others as a 4-week class that I built myself, so I knew it was not normal to have this kind of pain in random moments of the day or night—especially not so intense that it would keep one resting in bed for weeks at a time, not days or hours. As I asked for answers from the spirit guides and the divine guidance, their answers flowed through me onto the paper, sometimes more than one page at a time. Their guidance allowed me to understand what was happening to me and to have more compassion toward myself.

I sat down with myself for the next few months and slowly began to assess and question different emotions one after another. I asked the spirit guides and the archangels that would come from time to time to assist with understanding what each one meant and why it occurred.

In the upcoming chapters, you will join me on my journey. I have embarked on this divine mission to where I have dialoged with divine masters, archangels, spirit guides and the consciousness that came through to help me to get to the bottom of why these emotions were vital. Each emotion discussed in upcoming chapters occurred through me. I know there are so many emotions to access and understand, but what was given to me to share with you are the ones that showed up for me to write about. I know I could have made a thirty-chapter book discussing each emotion, but in this book I am sharing what I experienced and what I learned as my personal journey and life path, and each has a meaning and purpose behind it. Much of my spiritual time has been showing up to assist and propel this work to be developed. I am grateful to those spirit guides who came forth and assisted for great understanding to take place.

The first time I sat down with myself and assessed my feelings, my crown chakra pains, and the emotions behind them, the knowledge that began to unfold on paper was the path of understanding as to why such experiences occur. As the mystery of one emotion was answered by the spirit guides, another surfaced for discussion and assessment. As it did, I again wrote everything down. As I got to the third emotion, I then realized I was writing chapters on each emotion! The title then was given to my book *Own Your Darkness*, as directed by the guides. It then clicked within me what was happening, and how truly divine it is to listen to your inner higher self as it is at work through us. I allowed my inner higher self to propel through most of the writings of this book, and when it was time to step away for some months to rest and recollect, I then learned about a few more emotions that arose. They, too, needed to be assessed and added into this book before sending it out into the world. As the book closes with the chapter of "Rebirth," there is a realization then of what one goes through to rebirth the self through themselves as spirit, and a higher dimensional being walking this earthly plane, and the remembrance that it brings with it.

This is how the first chapter was born and many after that.

CHAPTER 1

Emotions

>AT TIMES NO MATTER HOW MUCH WE TRY TO
>RISE ABOVE A HEAVY LOOMING EMOTION, WE
>STILL GET DRAWN RIGHT BACK INTO IT. WHY?

It is not an emotion you are being drawn into, it is you *drawing closer to you. Not at all times but sometimes it may occur—for in some cases, we didn't know that part of ourselves—it may seem as intrusion and unsettling. Heaviness is just a phase one goes through to be in a position for transcendence to take place. It is a place where transformation takes place and new beginnings first begin.*

I will remind the reader that a consciousness is more than one, and can come from ether and space. Spiritual guides that have come to assist at times even come in a pair, or a group, and are sometimes just divine energy in thoughts transmitted from one astral plane to another to share the wisdom of information, emotions, and other things that show up along the way.

>THE EMOTIONS LIE BETWEEN PHYSICAL AND SPIRITUAL
>PLANES IN THE CHANNEL THAT TIES THE TWO
>WORLDS TOGETHER. THE POWER IN EMOTIONS LIES
>IN ALL OF US, AS DOES THE MASTERY OF EMOTIONS.
>BE MINDFUL THIS BOOK IS NOT TO PRESCRIBE OR
>HEAL—THIS WAS CREATED TO LISTEN TO GAIN WISDOM

AND SEE HOW THIS MAY APPLY TO YOUR PATH IF APPLICABLE, AS IT WAS TO KAREN'S. WE ARE HERE ONLY TO HELP AND SHARE WISDOM AND A DEEPER UNDERSTANDING. THE WISDOM OF SOME OF US IS BEYOND REALMS OF INFINITY AND THIS IS CALLED CONSCIOUSNESS, WHERE ALL TRUE KNOWING LIES.

As one activates within consciousness, such as Karen did, wisdom may flow openly though the self as a channel of the Spirit and divine guidance into the earthly vessel she walks in today as a human.

Emotions are where one goes to rejuvenate truly, as physical experience is a stimulation for the various emotions. As the emotional journey begins, one can access immense energy within themselves. The emotions are the powerhouse of the self in creation for what is not yet here and what is to be. The power of emotions may bring in spiritual understanding, connections, and gifts, and heightened awareness. Emotions can truly dictate our intuition and guidance in one way or another.

Definicity: a change to bring about.

"Definicity" may be a word you have not heard before, but here in the spiritual realm it is common. Definicity includes all parts combining into one to bring about change. Change may be only one action that brings one's dreams to life. As change takes place, definicity is in action.

Definicity takes place in sacral chakra when power is beheld and is harnessed well with direction and intention. To understand the emotions more deeply and what each may contribute may bring you an awareness of what the direction is ordained.

As I wrote this, I had to google what "definicity" meant and I learned that to have definicity is to speak of absolute assurance; a response needing no further thought.

I was in awe of how the spiritual divine guidance was so on point to give me a word that I wasn't even aware of, especially being bilingual, and how clear the definition of it is, and how it plays a part. I am grateful to all the help of the divine and those who are here truly helping and making this book be.

Karen feels emotions beyond this realm, where she may feel us or others as if in human form. It is natural for the crystal element in her to do so. Past and future generations have altered consciousness beyond human evolution and have descended to earth to be shared. Many will suffer painful lessons to create a help system for humanity and others will bring more enlightenment. For Karen, it is both. Both are given to be shared, as this is one of the creations of this written book. There will be more systems for her to create and understand why she is here. Do know that what is given is a glimpse for what she will share, for much wisdom she carries will be shared over a lifetime of her work.

Harnessing emotions may be the most powerful mastery one can obtain in a human evolution, as it creates worlds within the self. What to obtain emotionally is up to each and every one of us, as all of us master emotions in a very different way and can achieve results for our hearts' desires. Mastering emotions allows us to be our own creator of who we are in our own being.

Mastering emotions can be a pain but to utilize pain can be a gift on the journey to where one is heading. Be mindful, awareness can really help with emotional cultivation and shifting the right now to another, future desired now. Desire is an emotion and from there many things can be brought about. Each desire is different and is experienced by each person in a very different way, yet we often use it as the same word.

I am sharing my emotional growth and what I learned in my dark night of the soul and the hard-won wisdom it brought, through this phase of awakening, the power of emotions really helped me to shift the way I see darkness and allowed me to see how powerful it can truly be, and to understand it, and the purpose of the emotions it brings with it to experience, to cultivate our direction in life and what is to take place within ourselves, or our lives.

From the time since I have awakened, many things have taken place after that. One of the first things I noticed was that instead of feeling just me, I felt multiple presences at a time sharing their wisdom, dialogues and guidance. I see things that have died and are still lingering in homes, on people, or even the things I buy. For this I began to understand how important having symbolic things and possessions is, for I see the kind of spirits and energy it attracts into home and what kind of a character it brings with it, which then lingers, and we, as the human experience here on earth are then curious why a place can feel good or not so good. I see who is in that space, I hear them, and at times, the spirits can be not so nice and can bring really unlovinging energy to a place.

Waking to this awareness was intense, heavy and very messy. I began to be in more solitude and less with people. My red wine was my soother and this helped me to be more in my body instead of hovering over my body like a bird flying above. I also started to take more time off for myself for self care. When I actually would go and be in gatherings with crowds, I would use this to recollect myself, rebalance and release negative energies and spirits (if there were any) and ask them to return where they need to be. Some will go without resistance and some will beg to stay. Although in the work I conduct, I direct them and ask those who help to take them to where they need to, for I also have my path ahead of me, and need to focus on what is given for me to work on without intrusion. When I prolonged the work to release them, I would feel myself unsettled, unfocused, and unstable due to the discomfort they can bring with them. I know to some this may be intense living but this became my reality. As I pushed it away, the more friction I felt and the more I would become unwell. I had to understand to surrender to who I am by my own divine nature, and to be present in my new ability. As my consciousness grew and the way I approached life became more aligned with my highest self, I am becoming a whole different person every day. However, some, and at times even myself misunderstand why change really took place within me.

In my own experience, I feel I have lived two lives, yet here I am only in one body. This seems like the beginning for me and most of my life from now on to be this new version of myself in my element of the crystal, which was reawakened, and is on the path to evolution of a diamond. The parts of me that never before arisen have arisen and are equipped to help with what the universe has assigned. In my personal belief, I feel now in my awakening and after, I am being granted many assignments, rather than living life alone for enjoyment. If someone would have told me that they live by their universal assignments six years ago, I would find it so stupid, but here I am living it as a real example, learning in the process that when I listen to my guides, my higher self and my mission, my wellness multiplies. When I get off track, I get really sick and life force diminishes. The responsibility behind the assignments will never fail, as the awareness of divine duty overtakes and concludes on the next plane of existence. Every day I walk now with high observation, assessment in what can be more tweaked, and where I am heading. Am I to rest today? What do I need to be today to create what is asked of me? What do I need to invest in? What do I need to use my focus on and what should I plan? Why are there energies showing up here and what are they telling me? As my mind asks and directs, the other part gets to work to help with receiving the dialogues of divine spiritual guidance, of organization, direction, receiving things to create wisdom such as self help guidance courses, podcasts, this book, etc.

Half of my day for the last few years I would be in my spirit-energy work clearing and aligning not just myself but cleaning spaces energetically as well. For it's hard to be creative and to be inspired in a space that vibes low and is filled with stuff in the air. All this propelled me to live by my God-given purpose and by my higher mission. There would be times I would break down and just sob in my solo time, for at times I find it's too much for one person. Yet my higher self shows me how strong I am and I am able to be stronger over time. This includes guiding me to rest for days, even weeks, at a time, then continue again.

What I am discussing may not be understood to those who have not experienced the openness of heart I am sharing that causes me to go within and into a place of the unknown self. Those who do understand may have come across a similar path or have the same consciousness systems in place to go through life on this path. Although there is great pain in the awakening, one must be strong for themselves and pursue to the end to complete what is to be conducted. For there is no halfway point in such paths.

CHAPTER 2

Emerging Into True Myself

The emergence was one with great body pains, and high voltage shocks surging through the body from time to time. In the first stage I can remember, I had abdominal pains for years, like a knot in the solar plexus, and then the pain would shoot through my sacral chakra. It felt like a stabbing of a knife for months and years, and it would come in a phase of one day or two days and would go away. Then it would come back, and eventually never to be heard from again.

I would then have these pains in my root chakra. This I noticed after my spiritual gifts opened up and I began to feel myself as a different being, looking through eyes into a whole different world. In that process, the body pains were the most painful: feeling nauseous and going to the bathroom a lot, as the bowel movements would just be so intense. This felt like being in labor for days and at times it did feel like a detox of some sort, or a release that needed to take place for newness to emerge. The body and the whole nervous system overheated so much at times that I would be in sleep for days at a time, like a fever of sorts, not knowing if it's day or night.

As I lay there in one of these occurrences for days, several times I would ask Karl, my husband, to take me to the acupuncture to help to get the fever down. At one point we arrived at his office and I could sense how nervous the acupuncturist was due to my low level of health, but still he took me in and applied the needles. God knows how long I lay there, but the next day I felt full of life and my day once again began to be day, and my night began to be night. It took much rest, maturity, and time to myself to allow the pain to unfold within me and flow through me when it would occur. There usually nothing really one can do but observe in times like these, nourishing oneself, and really be aware what is needed to be taken care of in those moments——for what is to take place must first unfold in order to emerge into a certain state of becoming.

In those times, peace was not found and lonesomeness loomed, yet I took it as I must. For a human like me there was no going back and the pain was not stopping. Yet I knew at those times that it would stop eventually. The storm doesn't last forever and everything has its season, and I liked to think so do I.

As the pain began to overtake me, negative forces and thoughts loomed. Negative self talk was high and neglect took over due to exhaustion. Negative talk was not from low self-esteem, but from anger, frustration, and above all the pain that caused the negative thoughts to reoccur and activate. The need for sleep was immense; no matter whether that need came at night or during the day. When sleep came, I took it because my sleepless nights were many and I valued sleep when it was given. But over time I felt a sense of presence within me, a high level of peace.

It was morning and I sat down slowly on the floor and closed my eyes, sensing divine gentle guidance. For whatever it was, it made me feel calm suddenly, as though nothing else existed. I sat there for some time as my body went into a strong meditation pose and my index finger connected with my thumb naturally. Suddenly my mechanism for meditation activated, as if it was within me this whole time waiting for me to enter this state. It was bliss. That was the first time I felt quiet in my body after years of experiencing the storm within me.

I later learned that meditation removes psychic abuse, as psychic attacks can be on a higher level when going through an awakening into the spiritual world. For we don't just see the divine beings, but also very dark, not so friendly ones and not so loving beings that come in a form that can be traumatizing to look at. Some can come from family lineage unhealed that never went to the other side. This at first was very scary and intimidating for me to experience and see, and the only thing that soothed my whole being was meditation.

As I finished this paragraph a divine master stepped in and shared more on this… *Because it can take a person to a better place in mind and, naturally, when we are in a better place in our mind we feel better. That's because the body usually follows the mind. On psychic abuse, the mind tends to be more easily manipulated than the body, at times, not always though. When we meditate we can transcend our mind into a more blissful state. As the transcendance takes place, the attraction the mind does will usually bring better things into life.*

In my case I truly had to understand my pain and where it was coming from, then learn to transcend it. The meditations that I evolved into and went into when needed for relief were beyond the realms where emotions do not exist. It felt like all positive emotions were all there in one consciousness of divinity when rising into light. This place may appear as or simply be called "light," rather than an emotional state of being. When achieving the level of light within ourselves, light can be reached in the time we have with ourselves when in such altered states of meditations.

Be mindful that some will ascend through pain and begin their new life journey mastering pain and teaching from that place of transmutation for others to heal. They will teach others how to transmute it into something amazing, rather than be stuck with it suffering. As others have been open to light from day one they are born but also at times must go through pain to reactivate the light that might have dimmed throughout many years. It might begin reactivating and becoming bigger as light comes through, and though the pain will be there from time to time, it becomes lessened once the light fully emerges and is lit once again.

Then comes the ecstasy to be shared from the light within. As light becomes in a person, they will bring light to where light is needed. Many carry light as light workers and work with the light within themselves and others. As pain masters carry mastery of themselves, personal development, and cultivating oneself for the utilization of the self to become, to master the self is the beginning of all things where one is led in life. One must be prepared for where one is led or is to be led by the divine or higher self.

When one is led through pain or other suffering of life lessons and into life destinations, self realizations, and deep inner awakening, there usually will be pain for most of the destination until arrival. Pain plays as a force to push us into the creation of mastering oneself. Lying beneath pain usually is deep bliss, divine mastery, and wisdom—for when we are going through life lessons, we usually experience pain, frustration, and all of that sort as we become closer to our end of life lessons, our light maturity, and our purpose. As our mission emerges, and what we stand for, we then in the process obtain relief and there then shows up as bliss. The end result in bliss is to notice and realize and to feel this.

The questions I asked in the following chapters really got me shifting into understanding and propelling through the darkness. I was very curious and was asking to understand. As I asked, divine guidance would show up and let me understand the meaning of an emotion and reasons for its existence.

Why does pain show up?

The opening to the true self alone creates pain. As the opening opens more, the pain will be there until one is fully open and the journey to one's destination is complete.

What do you mean by opening?

The opening of the true self and the opening of the divine self, as two become together and emerge into one another, one must give. As this takes place, the pain will be there because we have much to learn from it as life lessons.

What is an opening?

One carries a higher divine self, the spiritual part, the awakened, while being the true self, as every day true living, and true being, as I am true as I am. The real seed without outside influence. As one carries the higher divine self to be opened, the consciousness of the act, of embodying the true seed of self, brings the emergence of the self into the divinity of the higher self, so that each may become what they carry. When this happens, the journey along the way may be painful. Not only are you giving up your whole being, your whole life that you know, in stepping into your own true identity that was assigned to you, and emerging into a spiritual infinite awakeness and higher self all at once. This doesn't happen often, but it does happen.

How do we know we are in emergence with the divinity of self that we carry?

Usually when one feels much discomfort in their body, and even feels a presence with them in their body, as an intrusion of the conscious that is taking a more active part in the self. One may feel suffocated in some way: tightness, and other such uncomfortableness that nothing feels like home. If awakened to this level, one will see a being of light following them trying to emerge with them as the light body. As they do, suddenly it will feel as if you are operating a vehicle as a driver of yourself.

How is it all happening in a person?

By awakening to the surroundings around you, which do not feel real to you anymore, you might feel you must get away. To spend time in solitude and yearn for quiet time; to understand so that you can emerge inward into your own world within and become present with your higher self to hear the higher self and to understand it more. As this takes place, then one becomes the self, fully embodied as that part of existence.

Usually mediation is a good place to start and other modalities that assist in mind peace to transcend pain and other sufferings, especially emotionally, which are absorbent positively to the mind and are nourishing. Begin there.

My Human Experience

The cocoon phase is a place one goes into as awakening begins. One usually keeps to oneself, such as I did. I was not in the physical world and was more on a very internal journey. All was taking place within me; all was waking up within. In those times realization was taking place, spiritual gifts were activating to be harnessed or applied in some way in this lifetime. For this, as I look back, I then realize I was given great solitude on purpose: to become comfortable with my new spiritual gifts, to know my capacity and have time to know my gifts. I had to learn to harness the gifts in a way that they could be used in a balanced fashion without other disturbances of any kind. Many feel lonely in this time of awakening (including myself) and especially of not being understood or supported in some way. It was then I realized that it was my part on behalf of myself to understand myself and my gifts. It is not for someone else to understand me or support the life change that was taking place in me. It would have been nice to have that, but maybe I was being prepared to know myself and my abilities deeply without others' influence. This took me into real inner self studies—deep assessments and to see where my life, my existing self, and this new part of myself was taking me. I wanted to know what it was producing in the process, such as a new consciousness, character, lifestyle, wisdom, personality, career, accomplishments and perhaps something more that hadn't yet been revealed to me.

After the cocoon phase, I came out like a child, learning the things I knew how to do all over again—to ride a bike even, to drive a car, and being human again. Dressing myself up in my own sense of style was a complex thing, but over time practicing doing these things over the months and years became natural again. My sensitivity to everything was at a high and this introduced to me a whole new world of symbolic, meaningful clothes, the environment, a new way of being, and meaningful materialism. What I wore became so meaningful to me and I became picky about my clothes, my style, where I go, and who I spend time with. I became ten times more aware of my thoughts and others' thoughts around me.

Having two boys aged 6 and 10 at that time of my dark moments of awakening was very frustrating because I was not able to be what I wanted to be, or be as I was prior to waking up spiritually and starting over. As a new identity, having relationships in the midst of shifting into whatever I needed to become, shifting into a new life outside the religion and of what I knew, new home in a different location, etc.––it was just too much. I had so much sorrow and sadness for the sake that my sons had to see me go through it and experience it all.

In this phase there was not much nourishment, and not much support given other than from my metaphysical- spiritual mentor, who helped me a lot through the process to understand what was *really* going on beneath the layers of all this suffering and confusion. In that phase I began to really study my self-care approach and my care toward my children and to allow new ways of caring become a habit. I made a commitment above all to rise into a better life: to rise above whatever was going on with me into a more soothing, meaningful life. Personal development was number one in our house and cleaning was number two, as a clean home creates a good nervous system and can alter it into a better one. In those times I asked myself, "If I left all my traditions, how can I incorporate new traditions that will benefit my little family and create a happy, fulfilled life for us and lead into a bright future? How can I do this without neglecting the family sector or my children's futures and above all their foundation that they will build on for the rest of their lives?"

After the cocoon phase, I then was going through a phase of learning to not be scared of my gifts and the capacity I carry. The channeling of the spiritual beings and guides was at a high level and at such a strong frequency that there would be interference from the other side when conversing with other people in normal conversations here on earth. The phase brought the gift of harnessing my own gifts and abilities, and being balanced in the two worlds, which took me years to understand and are day to day becoming more natural to me.

The darkness of the cocoon phase brought a deep gift of hearing energy as well. I was able to feel energies beyond physical realms where messages were flowing in for myself and for others. The guidance from beyond this earthly plane amplified the spiritual aspect of myself in such a way that I am now able to function in multiple dimensions at once. Not just here on our one physical plane or in one body, but in more than one place at a time.

In these times, I would go for healing sessions with my spiritual-metaphysical mentor to get more understanding of the spiritual part of myself and the path given in this lifetime. All during this time, my boys and Karl could see I was very frustrated in my process of awakening, for nothing was normal and at times my younger kiddo would say, "I want normal parents; I want parents like others have."

But for me nothing was going back to normal, and as much as I wished it would, it didn't and never will. What is "normal" anyway? Something that's simply familiar or common?

I know I wasn't raised in a perfect family, but my parents brought great order and discipline into our home on a daily basis. They both loved beauty and elevated their home and lifestyle with it, since both were very crafty and creative. My dad was a commercial fisherman in Alaska, built boats, and made custom kitchen cabinets from home. My mom was a seamstress who ran her own fabric store from home and later took on jobs in town after some of us children got married.

Expectations of the household contribution for cleanliness and order was high, and cultural and Biblical education was expected and was paid for by our parents. Both mom and dad expected their children to gain or practice skills or acquire a talent of some kind on a daily basis. TV inside the home was out of the question due to religion and my parents' choice, although some families in the community would have TVs secretly. A childhood without a TV had more time to be directed into other more meaningful activities like learning what kind of skills were bottled within, yet to be discovered.

This inspired me then to raise my little family with expectations similar to that. When I was shifting through a massive transition taking me into a helpless spiritual phase of awakening, it really took a toll on my mindset and self image. It took years to get back to my mother's leadership and to the order in the home I am used to. It also felt upsetting to see all the process and lifestyle built over so many years go out the window with nothing to show for it. This phase didn't last forever—every day mattered and did count after waking up. I made slow progress, but even seeing the slightest progress allowed me to continue to work on myself and my life goals and universal assignment, healing through them in the process.

We as our little family in the next few years began to cultivate an idea of what normal is and what is normal for us as a family without comparison to another family, and what we wanted out of a family experience and lifestyle. We began to add things into our lifestyle that suited the concepts of contentment and fulfillment, and made a bucket list to accomplish. I also created a motto that I heard from one of the Russian cultured women, as a saying: "If you don't like how I am raising you, don't do that when you're an adult. What you like, take that into your future and honor it as a family tradition." I know we are not a perfect family and do our best in being so. I do know each family has their ups and downs and so do we, and this allows us to learn and move forward in life.

Regardless of what was happening in my family and in my personal life, I want to share in the next few chapters what I learned. I want to share the emotions of darkness that had arisen for me to face in this phase of my dark time and the power they hold. The understanding of these emotions really fascinated me and brought more peace to me. By understanding them I could apply them constructively in a way that life could continue gracefully and open into light once again––and in the process have self compassion and patience. We must learn how to harness these heavier emotions and understand them through the darkness phase in our life, and to welcome the wisdom that can emerge within the greatest divinity in the self.

When I completed writing this chapter, a message randomly came in that I wanted to share with you:

Walking in darkness does not mean you give up your light and the wholeness the light gives. Walking in darkness is what creates the wholeness where the two worlds emerge and become one. Do not fear darkness because darkness is you, as there are many aspects to you. Only one who chooses the path beyond (the spiritual path) will tend to experience more where the unknown lies. We are here to guide and what was given is the truth of the spirit: darkness and light create the formation of life itself. The whole, as the sun and the moon.

I would receive these kinds of dialogues from astral planes, divine masters, and archangels at times showing up to share messages that were from divine consciousness. I then learned they at times don't acknowledge who they are directly but carry themselves as messengers and share what system they are from. There are several kinds I came across, such as the galactic council, consciousness, planetary systems, and such that I engaged with. A consciousness means there is more than one that is aware of this truth, and comes not as one divine being, but more than one. Sometimes they come in pairs, four people, a hundred, and sometimes over a thousand when the archangels come with their armies. It also can be an energy without a body coming through energies and fields, whether to encourage, warn, or protect. I am sharing this for the fact that you will see "divine consciousness" here and there in this book when certain things are dialogued.

CHAPTER 3

Depression

Depression is like a painful mystery,
begging to be solved.

As I lay in my bed at midday, trying to push the body pain away, I realized with frustration, "Wait, what if there is a message through this pain that I need to know? What if I ask why it keeps showing up over and over again and this time find a deeper true answer that is just lingering there begging for my attention?"

Maybe the pain *really* needed my attention and my engagement toward it, which I neglected and pushed away instead.

This area of the emotional experience was energy draining and I would experience it heavily, deeply even––sometimes for weeks at a time and at other times only days. After years and years of this experience I thought something was wrong.

At times, yes, there was something wrong––sometimes something was lacking, especially when I was feeling calm yet had heavily throbbing pains in my body and mind. I also had deep thoughts emerging that I needed to process and work through, and I felt the need to take time to myself. I learned years later that there is a pattern and the pattern wasn't stopping.

Through the pain, as my head throbbed, feeling heavy, and deep discomfort in my body as if there was pressure on organs, and feeling nauseous, I began to self assess on paper by writing down "Why does this happen and why is it recreating over and over?" I took the painful emotions that presented themselves to me, and began the process of surrendering into the darkness the depression led me into. Doing so allowed my heart to understand the true definition in my own personal experience of depression. What I am sharing with you in this book are my own personal experiences, and I am sharing them not to medicate or heal, but to share wisdom with those who are also on a spiritual path and personal evolutionary path.

The next few pages from here are dialogues with the assistance of a spiritual guide and consciousness who answered the questions I asked. It's quite strange at times to have this kind of access available, but I realized through this book that they were helping me understand what was really happening within myself while the suffering was taking place on the surface. The inner self was actually causing it and for this I am very grateful to learn.

What is depression in spirit form?

A form that awakens, destroys, and arises in those who are going inward. Only those who see this form of depression can experience the attitude of an arising self, which becomes another concept of self that can break free of the depression. It is a concept that one can master by going through it like a tunnel, yet even after exiting the tunnel still feel the lingering effects from time to time. After achieving the mastery of depression, its existence will always remind you that your inner portal to the self is here and is to be utilized f to go inward for true information and guidance. You can go into the self to obtain what is needed, then go outward to share wisdom with others.

What purpose does depression serve on a spiritual path?

What you have experienced personally was a darker matter of self that creates physical matter, such as pain. Pain is one thing, yet depression is denser and can anchor a human to self below where confusion can arise and pain overcomes. It is important to ask in moments of depression: How dense into pain am I now, and what am I to create to release the confusion and the pain of what is happening to me now? What do I need to prepare myself for what is new and true to me? Suffering through dense pain and the overwhelm of the pain can reside in that process, leaving you questioning what is to come, what is to be, and what it is you are to create. You are a creator by nature: you can create immensely and the density of pain can be a part to embody creativity. Then create from there because there is power in the denser emotions many don't truly talk about. Meaning: when pain presents in the path, at times, but not always it is in some way asked to create something amazing, or to release something and to rise into something, such as higher scale or potential.

I know this is not me writing this, may I ask who are you?

I am not human nor am I deceased. I have never died, yet I share wisdom with you of the darker forces, meaning the denser emotional forces as human level existence. Many think humanity can be a dense concept until they realize they are more like us than they know.

Meaning?

There is more to the physical plane than being human and nature in itself is dense. Humanity can be dense but not as much, as I explained:

humanity is a nature in itself—human nature. Yet in its own action, when one understands its own nature, one can understand how nature creates. Look around you, you will then be in yourself as a denser part of yourself—meaning more dense than merely human.

Do you share this wisdom with many?

Yes, I share about human consciousness and things that can be a denser format than a human, where depression may be resolved and understood.

What is your name?

It's not a name one goes by; it's again a consciousness. Meaning there is more than one. As Rafeal [my son Rafeal's higher self and divine guide], I come from your second son Julean who is laying beside you during this dialogue and senses this energy too. I am as an energy field, a part of his evolutionary consciousness, as he descended from you into your crystal in this lifetime. For when he was to incarnate, he sent you messages. It is time for work and you did hear and sense that he is coming, yet did not know what form he would take as female or male. The energy he shares with you is divine. You are a soul team, as you feel close to him and as he shares his ground with you until you become fully dense into a crystal format needed to incarnate to the next level of self. This next level of incarnation will allow you to create what you asked for and it will take time for density to take place.

At its heart, what is depression?

Depression is a process that allows one to express on a deeper consciousness level. Crying is also a deeper sense of expression and closer to heart.

Depression has been misunderstood by humanity—numbing it and running away from it. It is a painful, suffering emotion to overcome, *to transmute, to rise above and to direct into something powerful, such as a purpose and deep understanding of who we truly are. Yes, it may be heavier on the heart to carry, for that is what the heart tends to go through to get to the deeper realms of the self. Many may not know this, but those who understand depression and harness it for the goodness of accessing the deeper self know that when all the power of the self is unleashed, understood, and expressed, the self cultivates. Consider depression as you would your own car—it takes you places. Depression is so powerful that it can take lives and awaken lives to rise. It all depends on the knowledge, awareness, and the wisdom in the moments of depression that resides in one who is experiencing it.*

Emerging into depression is powerful but takes very high awareness to do so; to construct a direction into something beautiful and positive from such pain, suffering, and sorrow. Becoming as it is your own presence now, not later, this allows you to be with it face to face, and to assess it for transmutation, be the ruler of it, to harness it to your advantage, and use its presence to direct your pains and sorrows into a desired want, or goal. This allows one to gain focus on something and gives direction for the mind to be engaged with something. This then becomes the nourisher of it; become the pillar of it as to say, "be very strong going through it; be there for yourself 110% and from that, the light will emerge and begin to shine through the cracks, and heal." Healing is a place where one reaches a destination. Then the destination becomes the person, the healer incarnate.

To surrender to and emerge into depression, acknowledge firstly that depression is there. It may come in many forms, such as mental, emotional, in body pains, or memories—at times, all of the above and at once, which can be very excruciating.

Listen to your depression and listen to where it lies in you, for it too has memories that you can take and transmute or direct into something better. Be mindful that some stages of depression may take hours to transmute, sometimes weeks or months. This can be the process in the spiritual journey back to the light. Through darkness you are able to reach light again. Darkness can't last forever, as the sun and the moon have their times in the sky.

Inward you go, through the barriers and obstacles unseen, only felt in those dark moments. It is hard sometimes to share with others what you're going through, especially when others have no need yet or will ever need to go through what you're going through. At times, if support is lacking on one's journey, sharing one's depression with others may lead to misunderstanding and add more burden to self healing, such as feeling neglected by loved ones. It can even add more confusion about what you're going through as is, but proper emotional support is always nice and recommended. It can help to transmute the depression phase into the decided, desired direction and allow us to experience the healed part of ourselves more. Each path and journey is unique, some will need much solo time and some will need plenty of help from others for support and healing. Each journey is different and will have a different approach. Listening to what your own emotions are telling you, including depression, is healthy. It allows you to understand yourself, your needs, how you operate, and how to go about what you are meant to create with your inner divine.

My Human Experience

Before I went through the awakening, I was very much into arts, fashion, clothes, home decor, and home improvement projects. I loved designing and creating beautiful spaces, for they made me feel happy and connected to my colorful self expression that soothed my soul. I also was into the Law of Attraction and emotional balance, which I studied so much of, and through which I was introduced more to the light aspect of self. I learned how to be positive and how to attract through light—rather than going through darkness into the inner journey of our own self into our soul—the mission, and the true higher self within.

When it is time to emerge and walk into our soul purpose, that is the time we begin truly waking up from society's illusion of what should *be* and what should not *be*, or what is right and what is wrong. The moment I began my journey, I learned in the process that pain and suffering at times will show up to get us moving into our path, waking us up to our strengths and wisdom of knowing our capacity and abilities. As I went through my dark path into my true life purpose, a lot of negative thinking and emotions were surfacing and were amplified very high in those moments. During these times I asked the universe for a better way around this inner journey. I know one can't ignore it or numb it forever or be too busy to be fully present with it if one wants to understand why it keeps showing up. We must nourish it and rise above it. In my case I used energy work, acupuncture, journaling, and a lot of personal mind development to rise, which allowed me to go through the awakening in a more natural way. Again I will remind you, I don't suggest or advise this as a form of prescriptive healing—I am only here sharing my journey and the wisdom I received in my deep moments of waking up.

The information throughout my awakening journey I received came in as downloads and was channeled to help me transmute and understand the pain that was arising randomly. This meant I could direct and use it in a way that I wouldn't get stuck in that place of myself for the rest of my life, or keep pushing it away so it keeps coming back. It was then I began to walk into every emotion and see what the true meaning of the emotion is—owning it, being it, standing in it, sitting with it, and breathing it in—and know that, with time, I can transmute it and create an understanding of some kind, and I can create something beautiful out of it, then take into the future and share it with others.

Over time I learned when I surrender to my own heavy emotions, such as depression, the emotions don't stay as long. And like a car in a tunnel, I go into it, through it, and out of it. Usually when I come out of it, there is always something waiting for me, such as new awareness, new people, and new ideas. Sometimes I feel depression is a realignment that is taking place, readjusting to what is taking place next, and the more we surrender and become it, we are becoming the realigned energy. We are owning it as we are going into something unknown. I also learned in my case that I had to take a solo path with not many people with me, thus creating space so I could be with myself.

Here I am sharing with you a suggested Transmutation of Depression that I used in my process of transmutation and through given guidance.

Get into a comfortable position, close your eyes and take a deep breath, and then another. Become still and feel your heart's pulse becoming calm.

First focus on top of your head, or place gently a hand on top of your head palm facing downward and read out loud: "Depression, I am here."

Don't push it away, for it might try to fight against you, and cause negative thoughts or emotions. This can prolong the transmutation of healing, so be strong for yourself and proceed. By acknowledging the depression as if it's a presence not an emotion, the mind usually will go quiet. As it does, focus on top of your head, and read:

"I am ready. I acknowledge you, Depression, and I am ready to use you and manage you well, for you are here. For my transmutation into something very very beautiful it's no coincidence that you are here. I will apply you the best way possible and fill my life with good blissful things through you if that is the way to. I am ready for my divine true guidance and help, and those who are not wishing me well, step far away from me, and keep your distance forever, so that I can hear my own true divine guidance and the next steps into my good life and my true kingdom. This has been given to me to take action on every day."

Feel free to read this three times in a row at once. Take a silent moment to yourself and breathe the words in and allow yourself to feel how your mind-body is responding to the message you filled it with. If you even felt a subtle shift, read this every day until you feel suddenly quiet and well directed into what was meant for you. You can write this paragraph on a flash card and have it with you when you need it. Again I am only here sharing wisdom, and my journey does not prescribe or guarantee healing—if you need to see your doctor about your depression please do so.

After reading out loud the paragraph given for transmutation, on occasions you will still hear negative sentences of thoughts coming in after you have repeated the statements. Don't push these thoughts away. Instead write them down and if more sentences or individual words come in, write all of them down and keep writing until the sentences stop coming or you begin to sob. Sobbing is a sign of release. Let the tears flow and allow the heart to feel light, relaxed, tired, and perhaps even empty inside—–all of which is creating more space for new good comings.

Every time you feel the emotion of heaviness or you feel depression coming or that you are in the midst of it, sit down with yourself and listen to your depression. Try to get clear what is causing the depression, and if possible be present with it completely. Here, solitude and direction of thought is the key for transmutation and opening to light again.

Negative self-talk can be a human consciousness, another human's influence, a negative deceased entity, a negative force from a destructive realm, or guided information grasped from ether that is false and distorted that wishes harm. Negative self-talk can present itself when layers of false identity begin to fall away, and all we knew that we thought is truly us is painful to let go of. A lot of the time we feel loss, pain, anger, even confusion of what is going on and this at times may be why depression is felt so deeply—–it's a deeper emotion on the journey within. When true spirit guides and divine masters appear for the descent for the true identity and embodiment, a memory will appear as pain and activation will reopen the light in the heart. As the heart opens, many good things are presented and pain in the process, the negative, the false begin to fall away. You slowly emerge into the light within the self, and become more familiar with that part of yourself than you are with the suffering in the process. All this takes time to cultivate and recreate what is true in one's self.

Accessing our spoken thoughts in the midst of depression will usually transmute them into a higher consciousness. Here we will write all the self-talk we hear when we feel depressed.

Write down all the sentences that are heard while in the midst of depression. If the tears flow, let them flow, and through the tears, write them all down. All thoughts, words, emotions, and such. None of this part needs to make sense—just write all you hear and feel in the midst of it all.

After you have done so, allow yourself to be fully present with yourself for a few moments and just be. Do this for maybe 10 or 15 minutes or however long it takes. Just be with yourself, hug yourself, cradle yourself, or meditate and become very still within yourself—then engage in whatever is most soothing to you at this moment.

The next step is for each thing you wrote that showed up, ask yourself, "Where is this coming from? How does this apply to me?"

Answer each one, either writing it down or verbalizing it. Take your time in this area and be here for yourself as a true supportive friend would be.

As that is in completion, ask yourself, "How can I use this and bring more of _____ into my life? (Choose emotional words like bliss, harmony, peace, joy, love, understanding, laughter, etc. and work toward that emotion to obtain. Fill in the blank with an emotion, desired circumstance, or desired being, whichever applies best for you.)

Next, write down an affirmation. Fill in the blank: "I utilize the emotional ingredients I am experiencing now and create through them _____ in my life, now and every day. (Write your desired outcome, whether you want to feel better or to attract something, like a lifestyle, a relationship, harmony in a situation, fulfill a purpose, etc.)

Lastly, ask yourself "How can I start now to _____?" Finish the sentence of your top true desire that you wrote above and ask this question everyday to yourself until you see the instructions and guidance showing up for you. Continue to ask this question until you reach your desired achievement.

I recommend creating a flash card of the question, or writing it out daily in your journal to seek wisdom and begin integrating the divine plan for your life through consciousness and cosmic pathways. Give your mind something to focus on for that day.

CHAPTER 4

Solitude

> Solitude is like a gift, given to those who
> want to spend time with themselves to
> know what they are truly all about.

Imagine two people sitting alone in two rooms, one finding it a pure luxury and a treat, while the other one is suffering, feeling alone and neglected.

Spending time alone as solitude is something one must have an understanding of in order to indulge in. This understanding can also assist with knowing the difference between solitude and isolation. It really is a big deal to know the difference since this allows you to be with yourself alone in solitude as a luxury, rather than suffering in empty lonesome of isolation. Solitude is to be alone and enjoying the company of the self, and what flows through that time is a gift from yourself—lavishing in the time alone, nurturing and really spending quality time replenishing and rejuvenating.

Isolation is lonesome and emptiness, feeling disconnected and misunderstood, even when among others in gatherings. Being in place of isolation by some sort of negative force, invisible or not, can create two different outcomes and produce two different realities. When one is depressed and isolated it brings two problems to the table: being lonely, therefore constricted in connections, creates unloving self-talk, a sense of unworthiness, a lack of positive expansion energetically, negative inner thinking, and depression. This blend is not a good combo, but it happens, and I myself have been there. The second outcome is that this alone can scatter and drain the mind in such a way where there are no positive inner stimuli produced or have room to do so. Focus on some small positive components to truly become present with whatever is desired and transmute for the better.

Solitude plays a big role in self assessment. Taking notes about where you are in life, daydreaming, spending time with your goals, desires, future accomplishments, and transmuting energies of self to higher frequency or into a direction desired are all important steps that can be done in solitude. Solitude re-stabilizes the nervous system of healing to replenish emotionally and energetically. It helps to become clear on something such as a life direction by taking time to be with yourself. This allows you to know any area of yourself that you feel you previously didn't have time to know better and fills your energetic cup in the process with your own kind of energy—your kind of unique love that pours into you from your cosmic mother, your divine nurturer, and into your heart.

Needing time alone and being in solitude to heal and replenish is not selfish and may be very healthy to do. It shows you that you know yourself and can take care of yourself in such a way that you feel that you got what you needed from your "me" time.

This allows us to know we do have a beautiful nourishing place within us to go to when we need to, especially the time we need to lean on our own self. The power of solitude is the gift of learning to be your own best friend. Solitude is being in your own company in a way that it feels rewarding.

Awareness

Awareness is crucial when one is in assessment of their heavier emotions, wanting to transmute or get guidance on them. That is why solitude can be a beautiful space within oneself to go into, knowing that great things can come from that place. When heavier thoughts emerge, with nourished solitude we can hear them in a loving, compassionate way: our own selves, our own needs, our own thoughts, our own emotions, and understand what they are sharing with us, and want us to know.

Sometimes depression can be a release of emotions as well, and as the release of emotions occurs, the phase can even feel like a hangover after a big party and can stay for prolonged periods of time. One might think something is wrong with them, as I did, and it took years to understand truly what was going on beneath the surface, which happened to be a release of old to bring about a new self, and I know for each one it is a different matter, as mine was more of a spiritual matter. Embodying your deeper connection with yourself, whatever that may look like draws in new energy emergence that is coming though. Again the emotions may come repeatedly over time and can create a very heavy feeling of painful density, and will take days to process, if not weeks. Rest is important to allow the process to take place and to collect correct energy in a nourishing solitudinal environment that you truly love to be in. This can include your most favorite people and your environment, such as plants, oceans and forests. All have energy to nourish and replenish.

Intentional Rest

Acquiring rest is a place in one's self where one can go where the body is not needed. -Archangel Metatron

The mechanisms of humans have clocks and time attached, and the body, too, is a mechanism that needs tending. With tending one can bring great fruit, not only in physical form, but also in spirit. When one rests, they bring the divine into themselves, and can take action from higher consciousness. As the rested spirit reloads the body, one can create much more, for the kind of energy that flows through the body and mind activation is more alert and attuned to higher frequencies. Being unable to hear the divine in the self is to know exhaustion.

Why would a human need a clock and time?

Time taken, time given. When one takes time, one will give time and one will create in time as a human and as a system of planetary order. This all has to do with time and order, for time is part of order, and order plays a part of the self, and therefore the human mechanism. When I speak of mechanisms, I mean a system in the body: where time is activated, time can be deactivated. As a function of the nervous system, one needs to rest and to be in order with the universe. When one rests, all gets rejuvenated and the system replenishes for another, better self, which emerges from rest. A system rejuvenated and replenished helps one tap into the universe, including you as a human.

When one rests with great intention, one can create from energy not just action. One can create through energy, then the action will move to the divine destination. When action is not through attuned energy, one can be misled and attend other's soul destinations and confuse other souls' mission and think it's theirs.

What does this mean?

One can achieve things on the physical plane, but it will not be from their own soul or the self, only through memories and body recollections of human consciousness, societies and community's influence, and evolution that existed outside of our self and collected into self as someone else's memory. Few may speak about this, but I will still share: one can grasp information from anything, including plants. Whatever is on the plants lingering consciousness can take action on the plant as a guide not from self-soul. With a consciousness that is not quite developed as human, there are many dimensions, such as the dimension of animal and plant, human, masters, divine teachers, ascended beings, etc. that all desire to express and are on their own evolutionary path.

When one is disconnected from their true source, one will begin to lose themselves in this physical plane and collect into their own body-mind vessel and into the nervous system anything that is present in their space. That includes life, usually having lost the true identity that was given at birth and even beforehand. Without the connection to the higher self, the source of the true existence can leave the human body. If the body is not fully replenished or anchored in a way that it needs to be to receive from its true source into the physical planes here on earth, into our physical human vessel, to create or produce or even just to be. It is important to be aligned with your own information centers and receive information that is given to you directly from your higher self and divine guidance. Store this in your body, leading into your own soul works, soul life, soul destinations and accomplishing them.

This happens to Karen from time to time and now she is more aware of it and knows that it can and does happen. She entered deeper into her own soul, stepping more into self awareness, and taking more action from her soul and higher self's assignments—not from others souls or things around her. It is important to know what is yours and to nurture that which is yours by resting, focusing on yourself through your visualizations, meditations, and any kind of given modalities that assist with self embodiment and reconstructing the self. In that time you will reconnect, revisit, and realign energetically to the higher connection of self.

My Human Experience

Many of us, including myself, tend to mix up fatigue, stress, laziness, and rest. Meaning that there is a misconception that if one is lazy, they are not taking action and don't want great results in life.

Being fatigued is a lack of relaxation and means something is off. The mind and body are asking for rest and stress is a result of not taking rest to reset and reboot.

Even machines have reset buttons and cycles of oil changes and maintenance; so do we. Resting is to relax the body, perhaps from a long day of work, an outing, or something else. There is intentional rest too, just like when we set intentions for everything else in our lives. Intentions to go out, including intentions toward achievements.

As we go into our intentional rest mode, there are things we can ask as we rest and set intentions. In that time frame we can be more out of our own way, energetically speaking, intentionally speaking into our rest: "I am resting today, so I can have energy to _____. I am resting today/this week so I can achieve _____ and have better results in _____, and today I start with myself."

When we are in intentional rest mode, we intentionally accumulate the energy needed to get to the next step.

Many of us, especially those who are part of a large workforce, find resting a big waste of time and think taking time off is wasting time. But as a matter of fact, resting is a time where one goes within themselves and reflects so that their energy can be more in alignment with what they are here for and destined more of in life, as well as gently settling into it. In our rest time, this asks us to think and dream bigger, to realize from within something that we don't have time for when really engaged with work and our busy schedule. Consistent busyness does not allow realization to take place within.

When in need of time to rest, ask these questions:

- Why am I giving this time to myself to rest?
- What energies do I want to accumulate during this time of rest?
- What results do I want to acquire, after this rest?

Be expansive and ask generously for what you need.

Ask and set intentions. For example:

I am taking this time to rest and replenish so that I truly align with _____ because I want _____.

Make a list of what you want to be more aligned with, who you want to be, and what you want to attract.

1.
2.

3.
4.
5.
6.
7.
8.
9.
10.

When we rest, we are collecting energy into ourselves as a vessel of energy to be fully replenished. As we replenish we can intentionally collect energies to be more aligned with our own desires and life endeavors, whatever that may be to us.

To amplify the intentional alignment for what has been chosen, one must remind themselves why this time is taken to rest. As the rest period is taking place, remind yourself of the list from time to time. Read it and give gratitude for each subject you chose to be more aligned with throughout your time of rest. Let your body welcome the information in and absorb it well.

Consider creating an environment or going to a place where the environment reminds you of the list that you created for yourself. Think of colors that remind you of the things on the list and put them in that place: plants, candles, and even movies that will provide an environment for you to engage in rest. Think about textures to feel or rest in, such as pillow covers, blankets, or even wearing certain things that bring you comfort or make you feel your best as a reminder of why you are taking this intentional rest and what energies you are accumulating. Even consider consuming foods that remind you of what you added to the list.

Food and things are all energies and by being around them or consuming them, you take on their energy and they help to draw in that certain energy. Everything vibrates on a different scale of energy and we can really pick and choose what energies we draw in and what we want to experience more of.

Activities are wonderful as well—mild things like journaling, hand or foot massages, or even gentle stretches that allow the body to activate blood flow and draw in movement to feel more present and relaxed.

I asked the spirit guides: How would you recommend rest?

For divine altering purposes, be mindful of exposure to that which is not. Meaning, be in a calm attitude toward life, listen, and feel your heart; feel the time in you, honor your time in you, and then take action by breathing your time in. Although breathing, one may think, is nonsense, it carries many healing properties.

When you breathe in your time, you breathe in you, *as your own vessel in which you live. Remember when I spoke of mechanism: "mecha" means* you *and the "ism" means organism.*

As I, Karen, received this last paragraph I googled the two parts of the word "mechanism" and the meaning showed up as this:

mecha: a large armored robot, usually controlled by a person inside the robot itself.

-ism: a typical practice, system, or philosophy, typically a teaching or an artistic movement.

Now that you know what I mean by researching this definition and how I described this to you, you understand that there are both parts at play in a mechanism of human consciousness. It is the inner self in self movement.

You ask how to self nourish in times of rest to rejuvenate the self and your time in yourself: rest, sleep, close your eyes. Eyes are a definition of life and also need replenishment. At times it is difficult to just rest, for the body is in memory of all movements. Usually it takes three full days to replenish and to become. You ask me how: it is to be more still and less in action, for the reactivation of a new body memory to take place and mind thoughts to reconstruct takes time. Music, sound, and energy in nature do conduct as a stimulus for healing and realigning and for depending what in preparation you are taking in rest for. This is what you give to yourself in those three days, if not more.

If you are to take a task on evolution and work on a mental level, you might add mind rest, mind meditations, and the like when you prepare yourself for the activity. Energy yoga, energy movement to move energy and be in flow with your body movement, alignment during rest as sleep, and full rest with no action may leave you to be too quiet, while fast movement will be harsh to step into again. This is just to name a few. Take what you need.

#Affirmation: I have the mindset to passionately rest with great relaxation and ease and attract good things in that way too.

CHAPTER 5

Sadness

Sadness is like an anchor into our own deep self, anchoring us to feel more deeply.

Sadness is a place of self where we experience deep compassion toward ourselves or others. In the sadness phase we experience the softer part of ourselves—the nurturer, the helper, the one that has been touched by another's or one self's emotion of sorrow or pain. It truly shows the deeper love beneath we feel.

Sadness is like a river with a deeper bottom than usual. Sadness can be reached in those rivers that have surpassed into a bank of peace, yet the heart still will feel sadness. Sadness can be a blending of many emotions that linger at the same pulse as sadness. Mix rage and sadness and you feel anger; mixing sadness and calmness brings deep understanding. Understanding in times of sadness is what opens the heart to the humble raw experiences as an emotional human being having the right to feel fully. In moments that reside within that causes one to feel sadness, which can come in many ways, in many circumstances—yet the heart will always know the memory of sadness, once experienced. Once touched, always touched. It's encouraged to gently direct the sadness, no matter how difficult it may be at the moment, into something constructive through heart creation or expression. Do this as a nourishing method to replenish, mend, and heal the emotions in the heart. This will gently open the flow, and allow the love in once again through time and restoration.

I asked the guides: What is sadness in the spirit world?

Sadness is a heart in pain, which may feel more emotion than a heart in joy. Sadness occurs and the heart feels an activation of a new sense of being.

Sadness may activate and that process may open deeply to the self's authenticity of one that did not know existed in themselves. When we know our pain, we know us and our own authenticity for why we create from that place deeply and emotionally of beauty.

Those who have felt sadness are the most proficient writers who will write books, poetry, and such that touch hearts deep. Those who have felt sadness make music to touch hearts on the deepest emotional scales. Those who can help others at times when an average human being cannot, as if a supernatural gift activated to do so, have known sadness. Those who feel such depth can take others to such depth to share as well. Do not think sadness does not serve, for it does in its own way. Sadness is the transmitter of all things emotional and can create deep beauty, soul purposes, and a deeper meaning of life. One will pass through the portal of sadness into the depths of their own heart to access that deep emotion to create beauty and well-harnessed authentic thoughts. Each will experience their own sadness in their own way and will express through deep emotion in their own true way.

Not in sorrow but in sadness—utilize sadness as a door into the heart, for the heart yearns to express. For the depth of an emotion such as sadness may open a heart deep and share beyond what one knows. Exploring this deep part will bring more than one can imagine.

The underlying emotion of sadness is divine but not truly explored by many. As one begins to understand sadness and harnesses it to enter into their heart deeply, it is then they find the path into their inner world, the true divine, and the creator.

The message I shared was dialogued from the spirit world as I was questioning why I was to access such a depth of feeling in my heart, especially the past few years, to the point at times feeling aches within the heart. The divine spirit guides shared and even allowed me to understand more of the emotion of sadness and why it's a vital force. When I oil paint, I feel such depth of emotions flow through me and onto the paper, taking me into very deep solitude in my inner world of creation. The blending of gifts and emotions that I access in that inner world brings high-level creation but as I know now it was from feeling the depth of my heart that would fulfill a great purpose when asked. I also came to know my ability to write, and that is why at times things come to me to share with the physical world. It took time, but I became very grateful for the gifts and stopped pushing them away; understanding that they do serve a purpose.

Honoring something in us that gives us pain in emotion or mind-body, it can be such a difficulty to welcome when awakening to something more than we imagined could be. Yet when one realizes the pain is there for a reason—to create, to evolve, to flow again and transmute such as sadness and other similarities, the process can be painful—it becomes more understood and applied more with more intention to any endeavor.

I know it's not easy; taking baby steps helps. I have been there and experienced this kind of emotion for years at a time and learned that direct baby steps do create goals and help the mind to focus and have something to think about and take action on. It took me years to understand this kind of emotion that run deep within us. Many don't talk about them or advertise or share them in a way that contributes to what can be birthed in a deeper meaning of existence here on earth and expression into our own unique flow of creativity.

It is the emergence of the soul and for humankind to reach deep into the resources of the human heart. This is a depth that only at times sadness can reach and touch. Neither joy nor happiness can reach this deep place of ourselves.

The soul yearns to express deeply, and through pain, sadness may emerge to reach the depth of a heart to begin creation of the soul itself. At times, it takes many pains to reach such a depth of the self, and sometimes only once, which may take straight to the heart and go to the soul. Some are with it from the day one they were born.

Emotions of pain, such as sadness, may not create those things we don't desire, but it may create the most beautifying, mesmerizing creations of humankind ---if one has the courage to walk deeply into their hearts and know what truly awaits there.

My question to you, my dear reader...

How are you in pain---whether emotionally, spiritually, physically, and/ormentally---and how did it affect you?

What sadness have you endured? What was your creative healing outlet for it, if any?

What caused such emotions, if any, that you carry, which took you into your own soul work or purpose?

Regardless, it is time to utilize the power of sadness to create from the soul heart and be the force to transmute into something powerful.

The Blending

Mixing your deep-buried passions in times of sadness activates the energies of the self—you, yourself, who you didn't know existed. Through sadness, heavy and deep energies flow, and many are masters of creation: beauty, authenticity, and so forth. As the pain sojourns, it is expressed through your creation—craft, writing, and other soul-called actions—and then transmutes the sadness, the pain, the burden and releases it into forms of self expression and other activities to be admired and inspire others. It is then you have mastered your soul calling and your soul-emotion, which follows the deepest self that is settled in your heart, embodying your authenticity as the creator you are.

Remember that the emotions always serve. What you allow to flow through is what comes out, and this can be extraordinary and divine. Study emotions and use them to your best advantage.

My Human Experience

I remember from a young age I was so connected to my art—drawing, in particular. When I didn't feel good about myself or felt hurt or sad emotionally, I would always go to my solo artistry. It gave me so much presence to be engaged and all my sadness would transmute into my images so that what was inside of me would go onto the paper. I remember on several occasions, I would go into deep sadness and sometimes I didn't know why. But when I would take paper and pencil and begin to draw, my heart would open and I would feel my inner self being so deeply connected to whatever was flowing and creating through me.

Still today I go to my canvas for therapy and allow my soul to create. I know what it creates is from the heart and from passion, which makes me feel so alive, and that I have a purpose to share beauty with others and to inspire in some way. I am blessed to have a gift that I was born with to allow my soul to create and express deeply.

I asked the spirit guides: How do I know what my soul wants to express?

The knowing of soul expression is when we are engaged in something that gives us the most presence within ourselves. Meaning it will create a consciousness in you to be so fully present to such an extent that yesterday and tomorrow don't exist—only you, the flow, and the creation of what you are allowing into existence.

Some will take a lifetime to know what it is for them, some will know at a very young age, and some will have multiple things that allow them to fully be engaged. To be fully engaged in such activities is when the full presence of what those activities bring about in you takes full effect.

Most of us are born with a gift that we tend to do naturally, and it's usually the gift the soul will yearn to express more often than other activities.

There is also a timing for the soul to express and how we know it is by listening to our thoughts and emotions. Sometimes the soul will take an inward journey into the self before being expressed externally. Usually when the time comes to express externally, it is when one will not feel much peace. Heavier emotions will settle in, for until the soul expresses what it needs, through an activity or otherwise, it cannot be at rest.

Allowing the flow of processing of the heart over time may bring bliss through the expression of what was needed to create.

Finding Your Soul Expression assessment

For as long as you can remember, what came the easiest for you to do—something that you really enjoyed an expression?

What activities allow you to feel calm and soothed, and tend to make you lose track of time, leaving you in your inner world to create?

What gives you the most beauty in your life through your creations, activities, and so forth?

What do you notice in patterns in your life that brought you the most beauty, even in dark moments? What activities were you doing at the time?

What activities feed you and fill you with energy, even in the most subtle ways when you happen to be going through dark or heavy moments in life?

How can you blend the activities that feed you in your darkest or heaviest time to bring beauty into your world and serve your good?

This is a great way to know what can really soothe your soul and allow you to flow in a way that may feel therapeutic, even in dark unsettled moments. It's a great way to connect and be with yourself, fully and completely.

#Affirmation: Through my inner world I find my own healing beauty and indulge in it the way intended.

CHAPTER 6

Criticism

> When you know yourself to an extent, to where there is no room for criticism, you then embark on a well self directed path.

I asked the guides: What purpose does criticism serve in a general overall format, since it exists and does play its part in a human's life?

Criticism is a process that takes place through judgement to get clear on something. Criticism is the natural ability to express through one's inner self in a way where you can hear yourself and clear the paths toward a manifestation, life fruit, or simply on personal goals—and above all, personal priorities and values to fill your cup with what you want. Through criticism you can begin to release and transmute what is in the way.

If one is aware that in order to harness the mastery of criticism in a constructive way and better their life rather than distort and harm others and themselves, criticism can transmute worlds, emotions, perceptions, and create powerful changes that can shift the physical reality to one's desired aligned realities and experiences. That is how powerful the emotional life of criticism is.

When we understand why criticism shows up as a pattern in our expression toward the world or ourselves, our lifestyle or even toward certain habits, we then can use criticism in a constructive way. From there, we are able to allow ourselves to understand our inner selves, our needs, and our current circumstances, and do something such as getting clear what we want more of, or need more of in our own life. In the process criticism can diminish and provide more calmness and nourishment. The criticism begins to diminish back into the shadows, knowing it completed its work to show us what it meant to. We can rise beyond where we are in our current circumstances just by getting well directed in our own lives, and that is why it gives a great understanding on why we criticize in general and what triggers it.

To criticize anything and not resolve its recurrence of why it keeps showing up may leave one in a delusion of suffering. It may cause one to look outside of themselves for satisfaction, and it may cause the energy replenishments that lead to inner true fulfillment to be neglected and blocked.

Do criticize, but do it well. Do express your concerns and judgements, for sometimes they need vocalizing to take you to the next step in life, so you can understand what is really bothering you. Doing this allows you to understand what is underneath the layers of emotions that are showing up in a negative format for expression, whether toward yourself or others, even towards objects and life circumstances.

Criticism allows the knowing of what is wrong first before we can make it right. For what is wrong is the opposite of what we want or want to be, so to make it right is to begin to shift into a desired direction. As we become aware of criticism that shows up from time to time, whether from our inner judgements toward ourselves, toward others, or even hearing about our own selves that is coming from others, and vice versa, it can be painful and hurtful. But to hear and use that information to rise above that stuff can open doors to your true direction, to your wants, to your truth—even what you believe in.

This begins the letting go process of the unwanted, what is not yours to hold on to, including what others are directing toward you. Their truth and your truth are two different worlds and if they don't match in frequency they will unattach from your truth and go the other way. Such power can rise in all of us as we can master our emotions—we all have them and can use them as god-given tools. Criticism can be used as a tool to know where self assessment can take place within, to clear the path and transmute it, even to such an extent that criticism will serve you, not destroy you. When times of true self knowing occur, we are untouchable and we are untriggered. This is when we know the criticism is not directed at us and we begin to show others their own part of self-criticism for them to get clear on, as it can go both ways.

Criticism is a processing system, not a destination. One can use it as a destination and may be stuck in a life of criticism, rather than being in a phase of it. The phase is a powerful one and it can help inner transition to take place sooner, if applied intentionally in great awareness of the self. Criticize, but be aware that you do, and that is when you can take all the criticism you hear to transmute it into something greater than what is now.

How do I do that?

For a moment, close your eyes and go back to conversations, images, thoughts, and voices if there are any at this moment that are in the state of criticism and may have triggered you in some way emotionally, mentally, or even in body sensations. We can hold memory in the body and store it there as a file, so here we will open the file of criticism. Next, focus all the energy you have toward the sensations and emotions that keep coming up. Scan your mind and assess it; scan your emotions and assess them; scan your body to find where in the body the criticism is stored.

How do I know it's criticism?

When you feel triggers of unkind emotions, it may be considered criticism. Each one of us can label criticism on various identifications and here you will know what criticism feels like for you, as you will recognize what feels not true to you and makes you feel not so good. Note negative emotions or thoughts that show up, especially emotionally. As you assess these things that are showing up, you will also understand within yourself what is lacking and what needs nourishing.

What constructive purpose does criticism serve in the spirit world?

In the spirit world it is an ascension where all evolved come together. Criticism may have been their stepping stone to get there, as every destination has a stepping stone, and it does involve criticism in the stepping stone path. As one rises to the next stepping stone, the stone of criticism may be left behind, and at times returned to. Repeat the step to rise above and proceed to the next definition and what it brings, whether life lessons, completion of universal assignments, or understanding some kind of wisdom that is pondering our mind.

Understanding why criticism may arise in life or in any circumstances can really assist with growing, evolving, releasing, and harnessing one's life. Its purpose is to clear, release, and let go; to realign and become clear on a path. As this happens, it will create new emerging beginnings and new creations.

My Human Experience

I am probably my own best critic, as well as a critic of others. I know when I criticize that at times I am aware of it, and at other times not so much. Although afterwards, in my solo time, when I do my inner work, self assessment, and self clearing, that is the time I notice and become aware of the previous criticism I have conducted. I noticed this happens when I am either not satisfied in my own life, within myself or in my endeavors, or not sure what it is I want, and am in the midst of chaos, whether in my vision for myself, or in my life.

For this, I learned to allow myself to criticize and be okay with it because I know now it's a great way to hear myself and what's bothering me. I begin to harmonize through expressing and hearing myself. Afterward I do a self assessment to get really clear about what's going on within myself, which can take hours, days, or sometimes weeks, but it always opens up and I see the path that diminishes my inner critic. Then the inner constructor of myself reappears in my life to begin building my path before me once again.

Although, I noticed when I find myself criticizing others I feel great discomfort in my thoughts and body afterwards, physically and emotionally, as well as mentally. As I feel this discomfort, I know that is the time to go into deep self assessments and ask these questions to myself:

What are they trying to show me that I need to know in order to stop the need to critique them and myself?

What do I need to grow in myself and own in my life to stop the criticism toward myself and others?

What am I lacking right now that makes me feel unfulfilled?

How can I bring myself to feel fulfilled and whole again?

Gossip

Gossip is a portal to walk through to achieve realization, as gossip is verbal expression unrealized.

Gossip is the opposite of actualization—it is the residue of the unsolved and the connection to subjects of the unactualized. Gossip is the formation of incorrect nonsense that interferes with the process of actualization.

Actualization takes place when you find your energy valuable and use it to direct yourself in a way that it actualizes here on earth into your desires. This creates no room for questioning, only valuing your energy to manifest and overpowering the space where gossip could have taken place in you. Instead you took that space in you and valued it by filling it with so much well-directed energy and actualized intentional information and programming. Know gossip does exist, but it's outside and away from you.

I asked the spirit guides: Why is gossip here on earth and how is it of true service?

Realization is the truth buried in the gossip, the unrefined.

One will gossip or repeat over and over again to realize something within themselves to themselves or to others about others. Gossip is using others to reflect, to see from a different point of view on the matter. Everything lies within us, including self realization in many forms, waiting to be unburied and refined to the true purpose it dedicated itself to.

The more we realize something within us, the less need we have to discuss it or share with others, and the less need we have to be in assessment and be entertained at the expense of others. As we realize what it is we need, then comes peace and ownership of the self and the knowledge of what needs to take place.

It is important to know that gossip, too, has a frequency to it where cultivation takes place and can be assessed. As gossip takes place, criticism creates friction and can be harmful, not just verbally but subconsciously as well—ingraining it into the memory and storing it in the body and mind.

Gossip is a self actualization mechanism to take the next step into whatever may be.

When gossip is utilized to heighten awareness and to direct information to better oneself, it is a profound most constructive thing one may do.

My Human Experience

Even though I was raised in a Russian Old Believer cultured religion in Homer, Alaska, the home where I was raised didn't carry much gossip. When we would gossip my mother would always set us straight by saying how disrespectful it is and very improper; that we are ladies, we should know better. She asked us to consider how it would look from the other side if someone were to be listening to our conversation. My mother's disdain for gossip had an effect on me in my younger years and allowed me to be tuned in with my inner world more. I was so attuned to my inner world that I actually did not express what was going on inside me verbally. This created in me an inner self mind assessor and allowed me to be creative.

This also taught me to be very independent emotionally and to like my own solitude. I remember those years growing up, there was less conversation, more doing, more chores, less back-talking, more creative endeavors, and less socializing.

Crafts and activities I took on included embroidery by hand, which I learned in 4th grade; cooking from scratch, which I learned in 5th grade; and sewing, which I learned around 11 or 12 years old. Through all this time, I would go into my creative bubble and draw with pen and pencil, as well as paint. I was a curious, hands-on creature and was a quick learner too, as I have the ability to learn through practice rather than just studies.

Time to time I would hear my parents talk and plan on things to build or consider where they wanted to travel. They were really great at planning and setting goals, so naturally, their relationship was harmonious in that area of life and allowed them to live well. From my observations, they used their energy to plan and then create, not gossiping or worrying over what other people were doing. I remember several occasions they would talk about people in the village, but take that information and implement it into their lives for their own defined needs, such as to buy new things, consider destinations to travel to, or better their environment in other ways. They would use people as an inspiration for the better.

They both were more entrepreneur-spirited than job-oriented, and both had street smarts and old school entrepreneur investment spirits that allowed them to acquire well in the physical life.

Through that exposure, today I truly understand how gossip serves us if used and applied purposely. I remember when I began to awaken and better my life in my mid- to late twenties, I couldn't handle gossip because it would trigger too much emotion and friction in me. My sensitivity was at a high frequency and felt so immensely. But later, after a few years, I learned that it does serve a purpose, just like the message dialogued from the spirit guides above. I received a very similar message at that time through my awareness. When I would be around other people, listening and sharing myself, later coming home and assessing myself, asking myself why I didn't feel good about a certain subject that took place in gatherings, this knowledge of the spiritual purpose of gossip allowed me to know what I needed to realize in myself to create, improve, feel satisfied, or what to be more at peace with.

When we are actualized in an area of our lives, we tend to observe others from where they are coming from without feeling triggers and instead having compassion; helping them to transmute the energies by conversing with them with their soul's direction in mind.

Quick tips

Ask yourself: How can I use gossip––the information around me––to realize what I want, need, or know what I need to realize in myself?

Listen to the emotions and nerve-triggers when certain conversations take place.

When in solitude, go back to the information absorbed when around others and take it into heart. Ask yourself how each topic made you feel.

Each topic also has a frequency that may lower or heighten your vibration and emotion. As you assess your emotions and where the triggers lie, ask yourself the following questions:

Why does this call to my nerves?

What do I need to realize in myself for my nerves to be at peace?

What is it in me that I need to realize and actualize?

#Affirmation: I am actualizing with ease and what is truly meant for me to receive naturally.

CHAPTER 7

Frustration

Frustration will be in one's life when there is something in their own way to the destination desired in life.

I asked the spirit guides: Why does frustration show up?

Frustration shows up in times when there is a lack of connection in some way that is needed. When that needed connection to your inner self or others is not there, frustration may settle in that same place.

Frustration may also settle in for one who knows they can do more in life and are not currently doing so or are not able to fulfill that goal in some way, especially knowing that they can.

When there is frustration, one likely knows a certain area of their life where their direction is misaligned or is blocked, at times not knowing from where the blocked energy came or is coming from. In some cases, when we're not fulfilled in one way or another and we don't know how to fix it, and no matter how much we try to fix it or rise above, only then does one take a step or two backwards in life. It may be that the desires and goals we have for our life are not coinciding with who we are, and here again frustration may settle in and live. But as one learns how to align more with their desires, know that they are their desires and not someone else's, and flow intentionally into the direction intended, it may begin resolving the frustration in one's life.

Another example of why frustration may settle in is the feeling of helplessness due to having no ability to take control or express a feeling that cannot be accommodated.

What does frustration serve in the realm of the spirit?

When frustration occurs on the spirit level, there is an ascension taking place in other realms above or below. As ascension takes place, there is no ground to stand on, so the frustration is an awareness that something is not there to serve but to destroy. Many may understand frustration as anger, but it is beyond that—for when there is anger, there are also strides being made and forces being acted upon. Frustration is where one is in a place of no action. If action comes from a place of frustration, it usually is not aligned with the soul and is from a source of lack or blockage.

The soul yearns to express and when there is no outlet it may create an experience of frustration in the mind and attract undesired, misaligned thoughts that come in to create confusion and friction.

Frustration usually invades first in the mind than in the heart—for the mind directs and the heart creates, and if there is no direction, there is no creation.

To begin creating, direct your thoughts before you do anything. When you do, allow the heart to create and the soul to express by knowing and understanding where the frustration is coming from, and what it is effecting in your life, and getting aligned by understanding what you can direct emotionally or energetically. As the mind and the heart combine, the creation and the direction, many things will flow—not just energy, but every part of you in the flow called the present moment. The more present and directed you are, the less frustration can creep into the places where you are directing and creating. Do understand that frustration may be temporary and won't prolong further than you allow it.

How can I get myself out of frustration and into self direction and heart creation when I don't know what is causing the frustration?

Sometimes it will take time to realize what is causing the frustration. Maybe it's something you will need to experience to rise above and realize. We are our own teachers and we can rise above our frustrated self. By acknowledging the frustration, you may also ask such questions as these:

Why is frustration making me feel this way?

How do I rise above frustration?

How is the frustration I am experiencing now serving me?

How can I take care and nourish myself when I feel frustrated to understand what the first step is to transmute my life into flow once again?

Frustration serves the nervous system by helping one understand what to release and what to come into. When one feels frustration, it is important to try to be in a place of calmness so as not to distort the energy even more through planning and focusing on implementation. When frustration occurs, it can really take a person deep into their darkness until all is addressed. Karen has mastered the part where she hears the frustration, not only from the physical realms but from realms of opposition, and rises above such emotions to go into calmness. The goal is to not overpower frustration, but to hear it, acknowledge it in a way that brings to you calmness or a sense of soothing, and at the same time know where the frustration lies and where it is coming from. The feeding of frustration is the opposite of calmness.

This is a great inner story to begin with to nourish the mind and begin the path to a creative heart:

As I calm my mind and hear myself, as well as those who are divinely guiding me, frustration may be released where it needs to be. I serve calmness and that is meant to be, and those who wish not to be in service of calmness, I release you—for now I am filled with my own calmness and hear what I need. I am a positive expansion. I am my true flow. I see it, I feel it.

What if the circumstances and the environment I am in now do not allow me to be calm?

Being in a place of calmness is purely resolute, for it is the highest realm of the mind to be able to hear your thoughts and needs. If one cannot be in such a calm realm, then the emotion to go into is peace. Peace is not resistance, but allowing what is flowing though, knowing it cannot stay forever and there is always a transmutation at one point or another. As peace resides, a knowingness and awareness will settle in and will allow you to take action from a more aligned place of self. If peace is not granted at that moment, let it all be, for at times the best teacher is the experience itself. Perhaps it will not be from a soul expression as desired, but it will allow you to bring more desired richness into a future situation.

We can be at two places at the same time: in our minds and in conversations and actions with others. Not only will this allow you to hear yourself, but it will allow you to feel yourself and know how your mind-body is responding as the situation around you unfolds.

To walk into frustration directly, to be conscious of it, to know what it serves, and to walk through it is to master the circumstance you are in now as a lesson you are the master of. Not all lessons are divine, yet they do bring the result of mastery. The frustration is an emotion that allows you to hear what is wrong. To dissolve it, you will need to hear the emotion for what it serves. A frustrated person can take more action in the wrong direction than a person who doesn't carry frustration. Sometimes fewer actions get better results in the end. Finding alignment with a direction in life can release frustration in one way or another.

Frustration may come in many forms and may bring many unwanted emotions. Here we will do a quick self assessment and allow the mind to be given a direction. Ask yourself or write in your journal:

What does frustration mean to you? What are the emotions that show up around frustration?

What areas of your life do you find frustration showing up more?

What is lacking in this area of life that you think creates frustration?

What do you need to be connected to so you can resolve or transmute the frustration in those areas of your life?

What can you focus on now that can be just for you to appreciate, even if it's a small thing?

In these kinds of self assessments try to share and understand your destination of desire: a goal, a result, an experience, physical travel—even emotions are destinations. The direction to that destination is the planning part. Once you get more understanding and awareness, take the first step on that plan, and be open to how the next step shows up.

The soul's creative expression may release frustration even though sometimes it is not related to circumstances that are happening in one's life, such as artistry, writing, travel, activities of the physical, and more. As that takes place, one can begin transmuting and actually processing the frustration emotions—giving more vision, a heightened awareness and an opening, an outlet where the new things may come in making room. Then there is a sense of peace and calmness usually, and in my experience, I forget what is going on at the moment and am fully engaged with my creations. As we are more in the flow and as we are creating, we are able to think more clearly, so when circumstances come up that makes one experience frustration, emerging in an activity of soul expression, which is not even related to the circumstance will allow the flow in one's mind where the awareness will open up and give an outlet for a better direction.

Sometimes circumstances occur on a really deep unfortunate scale and sometimes we see a person is still at peace or in a sense of calmness—confused but calm, frustrated but calm, upset but calm—knowing the processing of emotions must take place to transmute.

My Human Experience

My frustration was very intense in my awakening journey, for I felt a sense of unfairness and anger. It showed up as why I was the one chosen to wake up and go through such big life changes while others lived normal lives.

The hardest part of the journey and the darkest path, I found, is to be a mother going through an awakening and not be able to be there for my children fully. At the same time, we were moving house, I was getting a certification in metaphysics, and changing my career. It felt there was not enough of me to go around and like I wasn't doing enough, yet I was exhausted all the time. I would do metaphysical energetic self sessions, clearing my troublesome energies on myself, all day long just to feel present, grounded, and human.

This created so many emotions of frustration and resentment in my life—especially the way I looked at things. I felt the energies intensely, which wasn't helping at all. Feeling things like fruit in my hands, crystals, or the ground beneath my feet gave me some relief, but other than that, the energies just took me off my feet, which at times were not friendly or nourishing. And that brought even more fear, anger, blame, regret, and so forth. I felt I didn't have control over my own self or my life. The thoughts that surfaced through those times were that I'm not supposed to be even going through this awakening—only older people go through these spiritual awakenings, so why am I going through this when I'm only 31? I kept thinking I should be working full time and living a normal life, like others around me. Obviously my inner critic was working at its best and was giving me plenty of thoughts of self-doubt to feed on.

Throughout my awakening journey, I talked to my mentor/metaphysical teacher whom I met while going to get my certification in metaphysics. I asked why this is happening to me, and also I wondered who else in his class of over 27 students went through this kind of intense awakening and his answer was, "It's just you and me." I also mentioned to him that I felt too young to go through this kind of intense spiritual rebirth and awakening. After talking to him, I felt even more alone and like I couldn't share anything much about what I was going through with other healers in the class. When I did, they would nod their heads with an *uh-huh, sure, right, hmmmm,* as though they didn't believe me. As I tuned in to my inner self guidance, I realized it was better to be more to myself in class, as there was no point of sharing with someone something they didn't go through and couldn't understand what I was sharing with them. But it was okay to have the journey on a more solo level, and they too are on their own divine journey and path.

A year later I detached from the metaphysical class and from my mentor completely and took the solo path in order to be fully there for myself without outside influences. I wanted to immerse myself in an environment that aligned with what I wanted and needed to be on a human physical scale. In that time I began to focus on what I wanted in my own life and what I need to fulfill in my soul mission.

As I was asking what the next step in my life was, almost three months after embarking on my solo journey, I found a lovely lady on Facebook named Carrie Green. She's an entrepreneur online who owned her own business and was very successful in it, and now helps others to do the same. I know I was guided to her as I signed up for her membership program and community on Facebook and I felt I was on the right path again. I would watch her videos on Youtube and feel present in my body and life, and know good things are not only possible but are coming. I watched her live Facebook videos daily and was on that routine for months, then I had an opportunity to meet her in person in Palm Springs, California, in 2019.

She was calming and very friendly, and the gathering of ladies was on a high vibration. From time to time I would go into painful triggers in my body pains, which was embarrassing but I continued to participate as much as I could. This opened doors to great opportunities and to see what is possible, leading me to really think about what I wanted to do with all the life lessons that I endured, and in the process made really amazing friends that I am still in contact with today.

I was still healing from the awakening trauma at that time when I traveled to meet Carrie, and was still somewhat out of it, but I didn't allow that to stop me.

I moved forward by being engaged in the online community, traveling as much as I could, and focusing on my business and what I wanted it to stand for. I kept going back to the phrase "helping women embody self-love." I would push it away, but it kept coming back again. Later I learned what self love meant and honored it more than ever. "It is self-love that takes a person places in life" is what the spirit guides always dialogue to me, assuring me that self-love is the fuel to get going and doing.

Throughout the awakening I always wondered, *If I didn't go through such an intense awakening, where would I be in life now?* I wonder if I would still be in the culture of the Russian Old Believer religion or be working in my own business doing custom design and sewing. Wondering such thoughts did create and hold frustration in the process to receive the new life ahead of me, and what one would call the good life, and being in a place of living a life with deep meaning.

#Affirmation: I utilize my strength and focus to direct the moments of frustration into the calmness that I know I have in me, and to hold the vision I have for myself.

CHAPTER 8

Self-doubt

Self doubt shows up at times when one is stepping into themselves of the unknown, yet to be discovered.

I asked the guides: Why does self-doubt occur?

Human consciousness is always evolving and so is the awareness of self and the relationship with the self. As one begins to emerge into a bigger scale of self, doubt is natural. When we enter a new territory of self, the new self is not yet familiar to us and that creates self-doubt about the unknown.

Self-doubt brings a deep knowingness of self, which creates what is known to us, resulting in a precise dimension where there's a sense of "I am self and I am here." An acknowledgment of the self is to own that part of yourself and create a stronger presence of self in that area.

Self-doubt may appear more when a new dimension of self shows up to emerge into and become. In the process growth brings about self-doubt, which is natural and can be honored as a new life coming into earth, as though a child from a mother.

When growth is honored, there is more self-compassion, gentleness, and ease in the knowledge that your unknown territory is safe, even if it's not understood yet. As understanding takes place, there will be another phase of growth, and another after that. With growth comes understanding and this is often a continual process.

When tested in self-achievement, self-doubt will usually be the first emotion to overcome. Quelling self-doubt is a phase to go through to birth trust and cultivates a sureness of self that creates the results you want in life.

Self-trust can help to rise above self-doubt and that alone will allow you to rise from self-doubt to understanding than any emotion in the first step toward new unknown creation of any sort. Self-trust is the power to harness positive thought by tuning in and believing what is possible, even in times of self-doubt.

In a state of self-doubt, you will usually feel a tightness in the body: an intense feeling that the body gives due to the fear of letting go. In a state of self-trust, you become something bigger and more expanded into. The bigger the self-doubt, the more intense the first step of surrender will be, as one becomes more present with what thoughts create the intense feelings in the body. From there, more realization can take place on how to transmit to the opposite of these thoughts.

How do I honor the doubt and the intensity in me now?

Feeling it through and walking into it, and holding it in your consciousness. Understand that it may be a matter of time before it will begin to transmute.

As you walk into it, walk into its presence by taking the emotions into your heart and holding them there. Don't push them out. Hold the emotions in your heart of self-doubt and as you hold them as if in a basket, deeply settled in your heart, and at the same time go to the image and emotions you desire and hold that image. If you begin to stray, try to come back to the image again and hold it until you feel a sense of release or transmutation. This process transmutes the self-doubt into a desired goal and a destination. This will also build a relationship with the expansion that is taking place in you and transmute self-doubt into self-trust.

#Affirmation: I go inward into myself deeper than self-doubt and into experiencing my own self-trust and true expansion.

My Human Experience

When I feel self-doubt, I feel tightness in my shoulders and tummy. Sometimes it takes me out for days and I need to recollect my energy to reboot. What I found interesting about the dialogue above is that they mentioned how self-doubt is natural when stepping into a new, bigger self, and when growth is taking place. I agree on that part—when I take on a challenge that is exactly how I feel, and usually it takes days or weeks to transmute enough to trust myself to take action.

When I was in a big, abrupt life transition of leaving the Russian Old Believer religion, letting go of the traditions I'd grown up with, selling the house in the country to move to a city, I had to trust myself. The path ahead challenged me to do so big time. In some way I know that I too was deeply guided to overpower self-doubt and fear.

After the transition took place and being out of the Russian religion and culture after two years, life was lonely. Most of my family would not connect with me at that time due to me being out of the culture-religion. This included my parents, and it took years for them to be in a place of understanding about my situation and to reconcile our relationship to where it provided loving emotional support. This took a big toll on me emotionally before the reconciliation took place. The experience really took me inwards into my deep heart self and in those times I was growing inward, there was so much self-doubt in my mind, body, heart, and all I felt was pain, more pain, darkness, tears, and emotions of heaviness one could not describe in words. But in dialoguing the message of the divine consciousness above, I understood that my solo journey was assigned this way so that I would know myself and my purpose. I now know it was all growth and is a natural process toward the next step.

After a couple of years of emotional heaviness and inner spiritual growth and expansion, self-trust began to develop slowly once again. I began to trust that I am on the right path and what I tend to call soul destination or destiny.

As trust began to unfold more and more in myself, I began to feel stronger, clearer in my thinking, and more present with my life. As I collected myself, I began to focus once again on my goals, desires, and direction. As I did, doors slowly began to open, and I began to focus and take action on my goals and dreams. I began knowing what I was being prepared for once again.

Regret

To overcome regret, embody the path of strength and welcome the wisdom of the divine and the true nature of yourself as who you are. You can welcome wisdom and strength to attract into your heart and bring energy into that area of yourself. Know that you have the strength to understand why things happened the way they did, especially when at times you may feel all worlds are against you.

To know your strength, know how you operate and what your ways to nourish yourself are, whether it's to detach momentarily and reflect, rest, or travel to move your energy that way you're not stagnating the situation or prolonging it longer than needed. In some cases simply use your focus, meditation, and music that inspires you to take action and direct your energy to transmute the whole situation of regret into an understanding. Take action and direct yourself more into your wants.

It may sound selfish but it will realign your mindset and body memory to a frequency that allows you to produce what is desired—even through feeling the energies that are still being released and knowing what lingers in regret. In some cases, regret can play a part when one may give up many leisures, lifestyle, relations, and things that are close to the heart because that is the time one may need to step aside to see themselves in their own light.

As for you, Karen, regret lingers in your heart area and tugs away at your own life—what could be and what should have been. When this occurs usually it is a sign of regret and judgement of the self. This also brings about great confusion and may disrupt fate and creation in itself. When confusion comes, sleep. Rest your eyes and don't focus on images—focus on the heart. As the heart shifts emotions, the heart will create a better image through that emotion, so focus on what you know now: bliss. Say aloud "My heart is bliss." Focus on the better image and then repeat "My bliss."

To overcome the emotion of regret, trust in yourself. As the heart trusts, the door to the self always opens. Self-trust is the energy field that keeps a person going and feeds the path.

When one doesn't trust oneself, regret usually shows up more than usual. But as self-trust fills the heart, the heart feels at home and there's no room for regret to penetrate the heart, even if it does, the heart will always trust there is a reason for this occurrence, shifting the mind's perspective.

The true underlayer of regret

The true meaning of regret is that its purpose is to harness the self's power. Although when one experiences regret is the time to rise into power—it is how to harness the inner power to rise above the wounded in our self and into the power that can and does transmute and open doors to new things that await us on the other side of regret.

> *By harnessing one's power in moments of regret, always know you have an outlet to rise, to work through it. That phase of inner work is where you will learn things about yourself that you didn't know, and probably wouldn't have known if all was dandy in life. As the amazing gifts open up, the inner patience will show up, inner creativity will activate, the planning will be divinely guided, and all of this shows up to help rise as an outlet to emerge into your future and flow once again. When regret occurs there usually is great pain and suffering. In the midst of suffering one can really utilize one's strength and vision to redirect and re-build once again. — Archangel Michael*

When one comes to a conclusion about the self's power and its capability, one truly knows the self since regret cannot linger in such a state of being. Knowing the self brings power, and power creates change. When one steps into failure or regret, pain arises only to notify you that there is more to you than what you see and experience. Fully knowing your inner self will illuminate and dissipate your pain by stepping into the knowledge of who and what you are. Remember, when such pain or suffering arises, it too is guidance. Keep going and keep learning more about the self. Be in your own true knowingness. This alone will bring great power and begin the revealing process. As such occurs, many things may shift in all directions for when one knows one's inner self, one knows all of their soul and more.

The path through regret is realization, then knowingness. That's when one will feel a certain guidance activation in them like being given a path to follow.

Ask yourself these questions daily when going through a regret phase to rise above into your knowingness:

What do you know now?

What do you want to know more now?

Do you believe you can know more about yourself and that there is more to you than what is being presented now?

If you knew something about yourself that you wanted to know, what would be different for you?

What do you need to know now and tomorrow to take action to get where you need to go?

How can I gain more strength and understanding to shift from my regrets to what is waiting for me on the other side of regret?

This prepares the mind and expands the energy in the self in a beautiful way and directs life into knowing more––knowing the guided path to take and what is to be ahead of you. This will take the step into the mastery of knowing and guiding yourself and regret will be more at bay, while self discovery and self direction will be more at play.

What is the divine gift of going through and rising from regret?

The mastery of the self. The portal of the mastery of the self will bring about the emotions and challenges of regret. Although usually given to be part of the journey before reaching the destination of the mastered self to gain wisdom, if cultivated, then at times when we are redirected from one thing to another, losing things along the way, it will feel like regret. But this only assists to emerge into the destination given, whether to be in universal assignments or evolution.

> *Mastery may bring about many challenges in the self and play a part in the self always, for we always are in self-mastery. It is a journey, even if we reach a desired destination in life, there will always be another to reach. –– Archangel Michael*

Regret constricts energy and dissipates flow of abundance. When one regrets, one may even feel lack, and when in that suffering of lack, one may grow beyond regret and become aware of what they had to let go of in order to grow into something greater—whether a higher self, a more refined self image, or a stronger deeper purpose here on earth.

Here I will share with you an inner self-assessment of regrets. I know the archangels shared more about what questions to ask, but I wanted to add this part as well. It's not mandatory but if you're interested in taking this step, let's begin.

Ask yourself the following questions:

Regret can come in many formats, so what does regret mean to you in your world?

Make a list of regrets you might feel you are carrying with you.

When regret settled in, what were the emotions that arose with it? What are the opposites of those emotions?

If these regrets were not carried within you today, what would you feel more of instead, and what would you experience?

What would you fill your mind with instead?

What kind of life would you want to attract in the place of regret?

What courage and strength did you have to embody to overcome the regrets? If you're still working to overcome your regrets, what kind of strength and courage would you want to have to overcome regret (emotional, physical, mental, spiritual)?

What kind of wisdom did these regrets bring you?

How does regret make you feel today?

What is the emotion you would want to embody more through the experience of overcoming regret today?

#Affirmation: Even if regrets come my way, I am aware of them, and use them to understand. I will transmute them into powerful wisdom and self mastery. For this I am fully present with what I need now and I propel resiliently throughout my whole life.

CHAPTER 9

Self-Forgiveness

> Forgiveness is not what we give to others;
> it is what we release from our own self
> for something greater to take its place.

I asked the guides: What does forgiveness mean in the spirit world?

Many underestimate the power forgiveness has when directed toward the self. The collectibility of energies are drawn toward the self and the power of it is immense. The energy is accumulated and felt by others who are nearby.

Forgiveness is a self-expression that draws in self-compassion. The mastery of compassion is drawn from self forgiveness, which evolves it into the state of enlightenment. It may be in physical or spiritual format, but may one understand that a person with compassion is one who forgives others.

To have compassion for others is to create a state of being in one's self as a way to show others the way. Compassion is to help others evolve into their own self forgiveness and into their own enlightenment.

As everything begins with the self, so does compassion by the forgiveness of the self. As one utilizes forgiveness to go inward and access the activation of deep self-compassion and to rise into self evolution, one may see in others themselves and forgive themselves in others.

Divinity at hand may bring bliss, and pain is seeing the opposite of divinity. When one is in a divine state of being, one may be more attuned to see the opposite of divinity in others as well and one may rise into such states of deep compassion that one sees beyond the divinity that arises in others and in the self. As this seeing occurs, there is always a path through and back to divinity.

Compassion is a state of being when one is going through pain and is seen by others through compassionate eyes as beautiful—as they know what spiritually lingers and is developing underneath all the spiritual awakening pain. Compassion carries wisdom that oversees pain and suffering and sees what is to be. Pain and suffering is finding the way and as one finds the way, suffering and pain lessen. As one becomes more clear in their consciousness, their aligned life path and endeavors emerge as a deeper purpose. There are many paths and many ways to reach the destination.

When compassion is embodied in such endeavors, the ease in the heart will begin unfolding and more self-understanding may come in. This will allow you and those around you to embody their own path in a way that is needed. As you embody your path, people around you usually do awaken to theirs, but not all the time.

I remember when I was still in the culture of Russian Old Believers, in my upbringing before my awakening of the divinity in myself, there would always be gatherings at church and in the family to forgive each other before Lent for Easter, as well as times before Christmas. They would say we have to forgive others before Lent starts so the soul can be more in a peaceful place during Lent. I did understand that part, but as I began my inner journey to my divine self and path, I realized that this teaching of forgiveness means that no matter how much you can forgive a person the forgiveness lies in them not in yourself. This is especially true when you forgive others and what you forgave them for recurs again, leaving you to forgive them again and again. Every time forgiveness is given it lies with them, not in your own heart. To hold this in your heart leads to depletion, energy drainage, and a feeling that something was taken by force not by inner self-empowerment.

As I began my inner journey, I stepped into a deep phase of loving myself. It was a beautiful part of the journey before I began to access an even deeper part of myself, my darkness, the awakening, and so much more.

As I embodied my inner self-love, I learned in the process that we don't forgive others, we forgive ourselves. Having to go through something, or when harm is being done to us, or we have harmed someone in some way, we forgive ourselves first to release and become a higher vibration for ourselves. As we do, the self forgiveness we allow to take place lies in us and we then carry that frequency within us, not in others. As we carry the forgiveness for ourselves, we naturally release what was needed to be forgiven with others. This allows us to experience forgiveness in our own hearts, in the here and now, not in someone else's heart, outside of ourselves.

We experience everything from the here and now, and this doesn't deplete our self-power or drain energy in any way. The obligations fall away and it is then we step into our own inner-freedom. From that place one can then share compassion and love towards others naturally.

When both parties are in self-forgiveness and come together, it is then there is great love, compassion, and altering of vibrational consciousness such as unity is brought forth. If there is disharmony in both parties or in one, friction will arise as obligations from another or depletion in a suffocating way, which will usually feel like constrictions rather than flow of natural forgiveness.

When one is not in a place of self-forgiveness, they usually will not be ready to forgive in any way and will expect forgiveness from another party to feel at peace with themselves, not realizing they have to forgive themselves. The expectations will be external, not internal or in a balance of both parties. When one forgives themselves, reaches out and shares that forgiveness from a full heart, rather than an obligated heart, to a heart which expects the forgiveness to come from an external source, this further attracts disharmony. One is full in both inner and outer self with forgiveness while the other is only with the outer. In these times, love yourself, nourish yourself, and see how you can be there for yourself to transmute a situation for the better.

At times the person will come around, but at times not. In the meantime, envision where you will be for yourself in five years, and see where that person will be in your life at that time as well, and see from that place of yourself what steps you need to take to have that harmony.

How do I forgive myself?

Acknowledging the pain and what caused it is the first step—including yourself, if you find the cause to be self-destructive. From that, access what is harder to forgive first.

The harder part to forgive is when one is in the midst of quarrels on any level of self and the mind can't think straight. This misalignment keeps one from inner calmness and inner peace.

When in self-assessment as you're scanning through memories, which may trigger strong emotions, assess what is not justice for you. Meaning, what was done wrong to you that is affecting you still deeply till today? What is not justice is usually what we will want to forgive ourselves first in going through such experiences. We must allow ourselves to be there for ourselves, deeply nourishing ourselves back to our wholeness, then to experience or go through what we need to forgive ourselves for. This can come in many ways, such as a relationship, a circumstance, or a situation. This may also be something that continuously repeats.

In this quick process of practice, find a quiet place where you can be with yourself and the images that will show up. Here close your eyes, go to a situation or a relationship you have on your mind that takes a lot of your energy that needs forgiving. Once you close your eyes, go to the image you feel you want to release most. If there are people involved in this part, remove all people and things in those memories that show up and truly focus on yourself only. Allow yourself to be forgiven by you, not by anyone else. This is to release yourself out of that memory and emerge into a better one.

Let's begin by putting your hands on your heart, fully feeling the heart, and focus on you in the memory that you want to release. As you do, amplify the emotion that still lingers that is attached to the memory. As you feel the amplified emotion, ask yourself, "What is the opposite of this feeling?" As the opposite emotion shows up, start repeating that emotion and see what image shows up. As it does, fully focus on it and amplify it for five minutes or so. As you feel the alignment take place, repeat the following: "I have released myself and have forgiven myself. I am now creating better memories in its place." Start spending time daily with this positive image you created in your mind and see what begins to enter your reality.

Inner Focus on Forgiveness of Self Journaling Practice

You can use your own journal for this self-assessment. This is another way to do the inner work of forgiving and releasing yourself from others. This practice is not mandatory, but I decided to share how I do my inner journaling on shifting my mindset.

I forgive myself for not being able to let go of some painful things that came my way in life. For this I ask my higher self to take charge and work through me, flow through me and help me release _____. (Fill in the blank. This can be painful situations, people, things, etc.) Allow something better to take its place such as _____. (Fill in the blank with what you want to experience more of.)

I forgive myself that I was neglected in _____, and I now allow the nourishing energies flow in and begin replenishing what I need to feel divinely full once again.

I forgive myself for lacking _____ in my prosperous fields, my life, and my materialistic world. I allow myself to be open to receive _____ and be present in that area of my life in the most appreciative way.

I forgive myself that I had to experience _____ in my achievements or in my accomplishments. Allow me to see myself as plenty and flourishing.

In my relationships, I forgive myself for going through _____, and attracting _____. Today I allow myself to begin cultivating the true love of my own divine kind within myself and attract from that beautiful place of myself.

I forgive myself for experiencing _____ in my creativity or productivity in the area of _____. I allow my own kind of true natural creative flow to fill my whole being and emit it divinely into the world in a true way.

I forgive myself for experiencing _____ with my elders or mentors. I allow my true inner guidance to guide me where I need to go on my own path with or without people in the most blissful way.

I forgive myself for experiencing _____ in my career or my role in my life, that caused me _____. Today I am ready to let go of it and ready to create room for better experiences and _____.

While growing up, I forgive myself that I experienced _____ or was negatively programmed to _____. This caused me till today _____ in myself or in my life. I do have the ability, the power, and strength to transmute and rise into greater _____ and _____, thus giving me a sense of _____ within myself.

I forgive myself that I had to experience _____ with my family. This made me feel _____, and still till today makes me feel _____. Even though I have experienced this, I still direct my energy toward giving myself self-acceptance, self-nourishment and everything I know I deserve, assuring great things.

I forgive myself for not being there fully for my health, neglecting it made me feel _____ and created the result _____. I can still make a positive change, and take baby steps to celebrate my health.

#Affirmation: As I forgive myself for everything, I take my power back and utilize it for the greater good. I feel full of my own good life, my own good nourishing, replenishing energy, and my own choices. I feel my freedom flow through myself. This allows me to be divinely connected and experience more _____ in myself.

CHAPTER 10

Self Hate

> Hate only shows us that we allow
> things into our lives that take away
> from us and depletes us.

> Hate toward one's own self may be the most
> powerful messenger to our nervous system
> from what we don't like signaling to letting
> us know that our energy is being depleted in
> someway, as a result hate fills that place rather
> than love of self that is actually an emotion
> that replenishes and refills our energy fields
> so we can feel replenished and full in heart.

I asked the guides: What purpose does self hate serve in the spiritual world?

Hate is a mechanism that is dysfunctioning in human emotions due to lack of abundance in the heart, or in life itself in some way.

Hate in the heart distorts happiness and health in all ways, and can affect many parts of the self. As one dissipates hate in the self, all can then flow through the self desired and into life itself. Using the hate processing method I will be sharing at the endend of the chapter may help with knowing where one can't fully open to receive to the fullest or feels depleted in some way, so one can open up to receiving love for the self once again. Self hate can show up in an emotionalin an emotional way, or even though thought formsforms in the most subtle ways. When one senses hate toward something, it is a signal of some kind to the nervous system that there may be blockage.

What is the deeper meaning of hate?

Hate can feel suffocating, stagnant, cloudy, angry, and can even heat up the body, creating sickness. On the other hand, self-love is a powerhouse that helps to transmute and rise above self-hate, as hate is a clarification on what lacks love and flow in our own life. Many misunderstand the power of hate; for it may unfold many gifts in oneself, if one listens to its signals to where to direct loving energy to transmute and positively expand and receive.

To understand this more, listen to your hate thoughts, tightness in the body, at times even discomfort throughout the body; notice your emotions toward yourself, others, and life itself. As you hear or feel hate toward something, focus on that subject that causes it. Ask where you need to fill your life with love in that area and what it is lacking that causes it. For transmutation, ask how you can flow through hate and into your own self love where you feel nourished and replenished to see clearly where hate is coming from and ways to rise into your own higher mission, so that things can shift for desired outcomes. For hate is a stagnant energy in a field toward an area of yourself or others and blocks the correct energy from flowing––and it can stay like this for years!

#Affirmation: I feel hate toward this, but I know I can recreate harmony and focus more on what makes my emotions attuned to my true harmony. I can dissipate hate and stagnant energy by giving focus to things that draw in self-love to feel replenished and full once again with my own kind of love.

Add this to a flashcard and keep it with you. Read it as much as possible throughout the day and this will begin the shift for you.

Being aware of the hate we carry from time to time, allows us to know what is to be grown and cultivated more in the self to expand to feel full again; as hate can make us feel and actually be constricted in some way.

What is the best resolution to self hate?

Self hate is similar to how fear works. When one understands self-hate and how it shows up in their own life, one will know how fear represents one's life as well. Although fear shows up to notify one that it's time to take action where the fear is showing up more, self hate shows up for the flow of infinity or abundance to be reactivated or to be realized in some way. Usually self hate will also show up as envy, blame, limited thinking, anger, agitation, and so forth.

Making a list of what causes the hate in their life, in themselves, in their circumstances, or in their relationships, can help truly shift this hate into loving those parts of the self. This will allow the flow to activate the energies that are needed to begin the feeding of positivity in one's life.

If it involves people you can't forgive yet, find compassion and how you can fill those areas of yourself and your mind with things you want to feel more of rather than hate and everything that comes with it.

Learning along the way

Many think hate is something to run from rather than something to assess and to step into, through, and rise. Just like other emotions, it's an inner power one cultivates and utilizes to benefit the self, rather than something to destroy or shut down. Hate is a mechanism in the nervous system that functions to warn where energy is being taken from and what is not allowing the self to flow through to express itself in a beneficial way.

When hate settles in, energy is taken, and not for the benefit of you or others. If one suffers and another does not, there is disharmony in the energy exchange, leaving one depleted, and one not.

The sex mechanism can hold a lot of anger as well, if not balanced correctly. One can suffer overactive sexual sensations and unexpected sexual urges that can last a long time if not addressed properly. It is essential to bring in more cooling mechanisms to transmute lasting relief.

The hate mechanism allows one to realize one's own truth and align with it more, and over time become one with it. Become your truth and the hate will begin to naturally fall away.

Truth usually prevails when hate or anger appears—it directs us to realize what is not true to us or what doesn't bring harmony or soothing in some way. One must realize that anger is just a mechanism to step into one's truth by assessing the self—by doing that we can call in bliss.

Blame

Blame is a powerful force to work with, as blame is a direction for what one truly desires to give to the self. Blame is cultivated when one cannot receive, whether on a spiritual, emotional, physical, materialistic, or any other level. One may use blame to clarify how and why they desire what they desire or need.

Many may not realize they're in blame mode because their energy is more outward toward others than inward toward the self, giving focus to others and thinking they are to blame for what is going wrong. When using this blame mechanism intentionally, it mayit may bring many desired things into one's heart and dissipate blame. As this happens, there will be inner peace and joy celebrated in one's heart.

Blame is part of the hate mechanism for it carries many parts of the self experienced in a dissatisfied mode, and it takes away energy and focus from self-creation and self construction.

As one realizes their hate and blame mechanism is in activation, one then may take action into the next phase of transmutation for a better direction.

Blame is being in a place where there is no satisfaction and no fulfillment. Thus, it is a powerful tool to use to change direction, and a powerful channel to achieve a clear purpose. Using it intentionally may bring great fruit in life. It can create strong devotion and commitment to your new direction when you know what is the opposite of it. Blame can assist to give you a better vision of yourself and your own life when you know what is the opposite of it.

Cultivate self-love and harness that energy to create change. Self-love has power in it where it has energy that cultivates change. As love is givenlove is given to a flower, everything is cultivated and grown to deepen self-love. Cultivate the embodiment of self-love through mechanisms of self-creation—create through your thoughts, visions, sounds, self-assessments. Cultivate through your wants and bring about the intention of choice and the intention of trust. Trust the unfolding and the destination it can take one to.

#Affirmation: I love my heart and my heart loves me.

Self assessment exercise

Self hate is what does not allow us to have or feel loved in an area of ourselves or our life; so whatever that may be, is self hate in disguise.

These writing and mind-shifting practices I am sharing with you is what I use when I am working on myself. A lot of it I used for almost ten years, which built and sustained resiliency within. I saw amazing things take place in my life when I would take myself through the steps I am sharing with you. This practice is not an obligation, but takes courage, so here we go...

In your journal, write everything down that comes to your mind that makes you feel hate within yourself—whether you've been feeling years of hate or just a few days. It is usually linked to situations we have in our own life. This is what I noticed about myself—at times, but not always, people were involved but when they were I noticed they were there to show me where I didn't love myself or an area of my life. So I would take time alone when possible and see where those areas of myself I was neglecting and fill them with the energy needed.

Write as much as you are able to and allow things to go on paper. Tears and anger may show up, but still continue and write everything down. Fully be here for yourself. This step allows you to release what was bottled within you all this time and actually see on paper what was in your mind and in your body, living off your precious energy.

The next step is to rewrite everything above that you wrote that preoccupied your energy as if you have outgrown it or rose above it. Whatever way it shows up to rewrite in a positive encouraging way will be from your own intuition as if you had overcome it, and that it's in the past not to reoccur again. Rewriting everything will allow you to understand what you need to begin the transmutation phase into the transformation and to receive self love from ourselves, and pour into areas of our life in a way we feel loved by our own emotions: our own self that flows through us and the space we are in as our home as our life.

Example: I feel hate toward myself when I think about this _____ situation. (Fill in the blank with any situation, which can be written in more detail.)

Example to rewrite: I know this _____ situation made me feel hate toward myself, but now I can see myself rising above this situation, and I see myself as a strong mature person. I see myself giving myself the love I need, and through this I am directing myself into a true direction to receive amazing things that are meant for me to receive in that place where the situation was taking up my space and energy.

Be creative with your writing and truly be there for yourself. Once you are done rewriting, you will feel a sudden weight lifted from your shoulders. Take a deep breath and feel how light your heart feels. When you are finished rewriting everything, read out loud to yourself your positive new direction for life.

Here I also added a few questions to redirect your mind to begin directing yourself into more harmony, release, and growth. They are simple and get the mind thinking and going once again.

I noticed self hate activates within me when _____.

Why? _____.

What can I focus on now to begin to fill myself with my own kind of love? _____.

What part of myself can I love to release _____?

What can I love in myself to grow _____ and to experience more of _____ (desired result) in my life?

I hope you received in this exercise what you were looking for to release, transmute, or rise and shine. I also encourage you to write here how you feel after this practice, and what has shifted for you.

I also recommend reading your rewritten positive writings once every day at least until you see things shifting in your reality. This will direct your eyes to see what you want to see and let go of the rest gently on a daily basis.

Affirmation: I am now loving all the parts of myself and my life naturally as well as choosing to see myself fully replenished and abundant in all ways possible.

CHAPTER 11

Ego

Ego cannot exist if we do not feed or cultivate it.

I asked the spirit guides: What is the purpose of ego in the spirit world?

It is not as needed in the spirit world as it is here in human consciousness and existence here on earth. When we are there in the spirit realm we are in a transcendent state of being, not egoistic as the human form is. We go to a transcendent state of being rather than ego, because ego has to be fed and to transcend is to be here, already fed.

It is important that both take part equally, as ego goes out and searches while transcendence goes inward and attracts from within, and is whole. Ego is more physical and transcendence is more spiritual.

In my personal experience, when I went into a deeper spiritual darkness, body pains arose and to dissolve pain in my body, I used a lot of meditation. Through these light meditations, my ego began to diminish, and areas of life that needed ego to operate and function well as a human here on earth diminished to a point where my human life that was given to me to live did not make sense. What took its place was a lot of astral plane living, angelic experiences, and seeing things on a third eye level rather than with human eyes.

What I learned in that inward journey in a transcendent state is that waking up to the spiritual world on a high level may cause a human to forget how to be human here on earth. The spiritual world is where the human ego once resided, shifted more into being very neutralized, very in the spiritual world and operating from that place. At this time, usually if you're familiar with chakras, you will know what I mean to operate from the heart chakra and up, rather than the full body chakra system as human, thus making the rest of the human body as a vessel of information, nothing else.

As one may ascend higher than a human consciousness and can forget a lot of the human part of themselves, it may take time then to descend, and redevelop an ego to its natural state of human consciousness. It will take time to anchor back to the root chakra organism to feel human again at least to some degree. If I could explain this in a better way, I would, but that is how the information came through to share. Even for me to understand what was happening in my body while the shift of change was taking place, was interesting to understand.

Without ego in a human life, one can neglect the external self, lifestyle, finances, and such, as I saw myself do. In modern times, it may be difficult to be fully transcendent and not anchored to the physical world. To be fully transcendent is to be like water with no ripple effects, as it's like the stillness of time, for there is no time, it is just there. When reaching these states of light within, it is important to anchor this light into the earthly realm and into the human body to create a purpose or mission in life. Ego is essential in that process and is to be cultivated, refined, or intentionally grown for a purpose in order to have the capacity to go outward energetically and take action from that place.

My Human Experience

Before I went through ascension and descension, I felt normal and healthy in my ego and I took it for granted. I would go to parties with friends, work from home, travel with ease, and do creative works such as sewing, gardening, home improvements, etc. It felt normal to take action from that place of being because it was grown from childhood into adulthood until the ascension began.

As I ascended from a human consciousness to a higher altered consciousness, life was beautiful—maybe too beautiful and it began to show. Maybe even people in my community and religion thought I was weird, but I don't blame them, as I would think that way too when watching from the outside, seeing this lady expanding consciously and spiritually outside the religion with her blue colored hair. Yes, I must admit that hair was the talk of the community and a freak show for my mother, as coloring hair was forbidden in the religion.

In that time of ascension I saw a lot of angelic activity, like feathers and colors, but not really hearing my spirit guides, only seeing them in my house and in my front yard. It was enjoyable and I didn't realize at that time my ego was diminishing and I was forgetting the life of a human. During that period, I didn't desire to do many things a human would. I would say no to social gatherings or find a way to avoid them if possible. I know I didn't drink much alcohol compared to when I was not going through ascension. Clothes and fashion for expression were not as important as comfortable clothes. Money felt like another language when I hit my light body activation. And I had to give up my stilettos for a couple of years. Imagine the agony of a human who loves fashion and was a seamstress prior to waking up! In that place I invested in a pair of shoes to be connected and grounded to earth and the density, so I wouldn't feel like a yo yo coming in and out of my body and would feel safe in my body while going through body changes.

Music was my favorite thing to engage with and listen to. I didn't watch much TV at that time, other than studying, and intentional visual time. I did a lot of studies on chakras, astral realms, galactic existence, essential oils, god particle, pressure points on acupressure, the nervous system, earthing, zodiac cell salts, herbs for drinking, yoga, and reading books on divine masters who also had to awaken and live life on this scale. I then also spent summer months sitting outside just observing things in nature, allowing the process of change within to take place.

As I began my descension, that became a whole different story. I went into a place in my mind one would describe as a black place where death and life connected, like a tunnel not going into the light or leading back to life here on earth. It was just dark and an unknown part of myself was unfolding and at times it was something I couldn't bear.

I had just gotten out of the third semester of my metaphysical school, which was five days each week and two hours of driving from home to the location. When the descension began, it was springtime. I felt energy from everywhere; it was intense, but I was able to go outside in that season and connect with the tree roots. This helped me to be stable and feel calm, whether at midnight or during the day. The color green was very nourishing, therapeutic, and lush. By the time my descension experience was amplified, I felt at times like I was sucked out of my body into the sky by a vacuum. Then I would feel a presence entering my body, like an energy of some sort. It was so hard because it would happen randomly and it was very difficult to ground the energies that were with me during that time.

The first step I experienced on an extreme level was to descend back into my crown chakra, which really kept me ungrounded for a year plus. Through that phase, it made me think all these thoughts of not knowing who I am, why this was happening to me, and wondering if it will be like this forever. The whole experience of descension was the scariest, most traumatic thing for me. What helped was taking my two boys to a nearby lake to be by water and just to listen to simple things like birds singing and laughter from afar, water splashing and delighted squeals. All those little things mattered and did make a difference.

As I was descending lower into my body chakras, I began to have different needs in life, as I had to study my human nature, and its new needs. My clothes became symbolic: the texture of clothes was super important, as each texture brought a different vibration to experience. My food taste changed to more dense foods with red wine on the side. Money began to show up as important once again and felt natural. TV time opened up and I began to watch more of it in order to be engaged with something rather than my descension. In those times, I was very moody and hyper-sensitive, yet was aware that I was—not just to people but things. I would stand by a non-living object and feel the vibration of it, as if it was alive. I learned through my own experience that everything is energy. This concept of existence took a while for me to get used to.

I became more picky about where I went and what I did, as in activities, entertainment, or on a day-to-day basis. Everything I did was meaningful and felt more deeply, knowing each action produced health, identity, and contribution to the human consciousness to the new generations. All things I took action on was contributional to human evolution, and this includes daily grooming my two sons and my husband Karl on how life is deep and meaningful. At times they would feel I was overwhelming them with information, but the downloads of information to share with them came at a rapid speed and with a lot of information at a time. If I wasn't going through such a major inner shift, I would never teach any personal development and self care to our children. At times I feel it was destiny and was asked of me.

The transition back into full descension was a few years and today I feel my root chakra readjusting and clicking back to my own reality. In this process I did receive messages from my divine guidance and spiritual team about how to do self care and what to do to humanitize my ego in a healthy way. That included getting acquainted with economics, money, and materialistic value, how to go about a daily routine, how to master dialogues where I am in control of it, not vice versa––and above all, build and attract deep true relationships that are very healing, nourishing, loving, kind and gentle. Meaning they are very understanding and compassionate; asking mindfully and attracting mutual relationships.

As I began to feed my ego after descending more than halfway, I then began to cultivate it and define it for what I wanted my ego to stand for in the external part of my inner self in this world. I considered what I wanted more of in my life––specifically what I wanted to feel more of, which was more beauty, more purpose, more meaning, more harmony, more soothing, and more calmness. That was the period where I spent more time in deep meditations and personal development. That was also when my gifts opened up to dialogue with the divine and others from spirit lands and realms. That took me over a year to get used to and I still am getting used to it. I needed to reframe my idea of being and living, and be comfortable with it. My spiritual mentor was very gifted in that department and guided me through my fears to understand a deeper meaning of what was really happening, until I had to go on on my solo spiritual path.

As I descended more into my life, I learned I have to feed my ego all the time. When I wouldn't feed it, I would go back into nothingness and become everything all at once, losing my human identity and the whole perception of my existence.

Take Care

After the descension, I studied myself like a book afterwards, considering my new life habits and the new needs of my new daily life. I learned what kind of affirmative music needed to be on for the night, which was more of a white noise to replenish the body, and beach waves, for the beach is soothing and relaxes my body deeply. When I would do that, the second morning after waking up I would feel more human and more present. I would even forget I was still going through my spiritual awakening. When I would not turn the music on, the next day I would get back to square one, feeling ungrounded and not in my body, along with seeing and feeling things I didn't want to.

I made a habit of doing a nightly affirmation each evening such as, "I am rooted into my own foot chakras, I feel safe here on earth. I am now whole again and feel myself fully healed." I was guided to watch more soothing movies to do intentional imaging, that way self-projection would be more enjoyable. I usually would pick Hallmark movies that suited the lifestyle I wanted to embody. The reality shows worked as well because I would engage in their lives and feel more connected on a human scale.

I also began to drink alcohol again, which I didn't drink over a two to three-year period. I realized it can numb the hyper-sensitivity and ground me to the earthly experience, even allowing me to feel normal. I stuck to red wines, which I learned were very grounding and relaxed the body more than the white wine.

I felt like I was relearning how to take care of myself in a whole new way and that never really stopped. Even today I still find a way to tweak my self-care to feel more soothed in my body and to ease the pain of descenion.

During this phase of learning to feed and care for the ego part of myself, the part I found most frustrating is that I couldn't do what I wanted, when I wanted, as the self-care was so strict. I felt like I was the mother to a child of myself, experiencing both in one at the same time. As my two children and my husband watched me without being able to help, since everything was shifting from the inside for me, I knew I didn't want to live like this forever. To prepare for exiting this stage, I really loaded myself up with mind audio music and repeated affirmations over and over again. I wrote my affirmations on flashcards and did yoga and deep meditations. A lot of camping was refreshing as well, so thank god it was summer by this point. This shift took me more into enlightenment and bliss, something that was so opposite of all the pain I went through. I then realized that

Own Your Darkness

is how it is to have the awakening happen not just physically but spiritually as well.

> *When one goes through such consciousness awareness as Karen did, there are many lessons she went through that are indescribable, yet they are felt and remembered as if it was yesterday. The pain is immense and some even don't make it through alive till the end. Karen did, for she had strength, wisdom, and so much help from her spiritual family, as well as spirits who are not incarnate in physical bodies. They would say "you were never alone," reminding her from time to time. Still, she felt so alone and that life was not fair, especially when she had to leave her physical family and move to a place where she had to endure her path solo. This brought more pain as she felt burdened with the universal assignment to awaken and serve from a place of her higher self. She felt angry with herself and with the pains she had to go through mostly alone, and not truly have the support needed for a human. The spirit guides were always with her but she needed more, for she was in a lesson of self-care in a powerful state of being: to evolve and help others awaken on such a deep scale of the self as well. Not all are called to awaken to such a depth of the self, but she is a rare breed and it was her destiny. -- Archangel Michael*

#Affirmation: My ego is an essential part of me, and as it fills my cup with my own kind of existance, it then flows and nourishes all areas of my life.

CHAPTER 12

The snob in us

Snobbery system: The scaled high self; a level to rise to, at times into a system of inner self, to where one is to *be* of what needs to take part as fruit in the physical life.

I asked the spirit guides: Why is being a snob essential and when does it serve?

The kind of snobetory system we are talking about here is to rise above yourself into a higher self where you need to be to vibrate at a certain vibration to create, and diminish all that cannot.

Snobbery systems are when one has a clear definition in life and practices them to such an extent where there is no room for anything else. High level achievements begin to diminish as one lowers their standards to please others, potential disintegrates, and disvalue occurs.

Snobbery is a portal into a synthesis where all is well and created. When one understands snobbery, it may repel things one doesn't want in their own life. When creating healthy boundaries with others, snobbery is essential to create the life desired. When snobbery is in full effect, it may give many things at once.

After I channeled the paragraph above, I had to google the definition of synthesis. It came up as "a combination of created theory or system."

It's just like baking a cake. When you bake a cake, you only need certain ingredients and in certain doses. If one is to make a cake when there are no certain ingredients in mind, just random ones with no certain doses, the result will be different than when using certain ingredients and in certain doses intentionally to produce a desired result.

How can snobbery be achieved to better a life?

Mastery through emotions as we are sharing in this book. You may be able to understand your emotions more and in some way and find the pain as a messenger, as pain can cultivate wisdom and self-snobbery can cultivate high value of the self on a different frequency. Snobbery, if used constructively, is a divine essence in itself. It creates an identity of formation as a way of harnessing self-creation.

I knew myself and valued myself, and as I did, I was able to create mastery through myself in my works. When one creates a high mastery of the self, there is a snobbish essence about the creation, for much value was put into the work. I had to master my emotions when in training, and as I did, I began to value my time and became more mindful of who and what I allowed into my life. This allows me to fulfill what I came here to do as a mission and a purpose. I know some might think it's selfish and actually snobby to do so, but again think how things are made with a certain approach, a certain skill, and a certain vibration and production—everything produces in a way how it was put into production. If one wants precise production in anything, one must also think or even ask within to have the correct ingredients and resources, and for the rest to fall away in order to produce the highest quality.

Life is time and time is life, thus valued time creates a valued life. Not many understand that valuing time is a sense of snobbery and plays a great part in creating from one's higher self. As one creates on such a high scale of self, snobbery is needed to be in the state of mind to create and formulate. When there is no sense of snobbery involved, many things can come in and distort a creation of what was to be, and at times make it so that the work is not able to be created or completed. Snobbery is effective and if used in a constructive way, it may bring many fruits.

Snobbery is not pushing away things—snobbery is creating space for the things one values in one's life. Snobbery is not to hurt or look down on others, it is to value and distance oneself to spend time with one's inner self and with inner divine creations, as an assignment from the divine, works, and mastery. Snobbery is a divine thing where we all come from and attunement to snobbery is bliss. As bliss is obtained, one may enjoy their own company and their works, for nothing comes before that. Snobbery can be achieved through one's works and mind, then it is a portal one goes through to obtain achievements of the self and to create on a higher divine scale.

High scales one can master through practicing is focus and dedication. As these are established, it may foster momentum for more creations and a deep knowingness in one's heart desired value to produce high quality. Through that, one attunes themselves, receives divine guidance from higher self or from the infinite source and gives the mind direction, then creates here on earth. As creation takes place, a frequency is achieved and a certain flow is established. As this happens, a new identity of self emerges and snobbery is experienced, as the creation then comes to life through that flow of high level of quality.

Is it egotistic speaking of such snobbery?

Not necessarily when one understands the high levels of existence of their own self. Spiritual snobbery is different from being rude or unkind. Snobbery is valuing the self, where one directs oneself to such an extent where there is no room for anything else. Filling your schedule with your universal assignments, filling your day with great goals of the day and descipline toward the work, being one with it, breathing it, being it, living it; as it is you, you are your creation and the extension of it in your production. Ego is not snobbery because snobbery lies in a person's altered state of being and path of sharing themselves on a certain frequency with the world. When understood and used properly, and applied intentionally, snobbery can be immensely valuable.

Being a snob is being concrete in life to such an extent where you are giving prioritized attention knowing how valuable your energy is. To achieve or become or maintain by mastering this part of one's self allows you to see and take yourself out of a place or situation that's not valuable to you and is not giving back in any way. Snobbery is an identity and a flow frequency of one's life. Not all lives need to be on high a snobbery system, for not all are asked to achieve a high value of self mastery to create. Only those who are asked will tend to carry this identity more than usual on a day-to-day basis. It is the nature of being. If one chooses a snobbery system and develops it well in a constructive form within themselves, one can give and create of themselves on that scale.

Environment

People and things are a creation of the environment. When I was still in the Russian religion, it programmed me for who I was to be then. As I left religion due to my spiritual awakening and energy work, I had to expose myself to other worlds, such as the secular Americanized culture and healers' worlds, and it made me a different person. When I was around people who practiced self-care and personally developed, I saw the best version of myself. As I engaged with people who didn't do self-care and didn't personally develop, I saw heaviness in myself and would stop my own self-care, which led to neglect. I would get moody and agitated. My routine would be off and it would take me days, if not weeks, to realign and get back on track for what I needed to create and produce again.

I then began to assess and notice there were patterns among the people that I socialized with and the things I surrounded myself with. As I did, I began to be more mindful and aware where and what I expose myself to. I know my self care creates my lifestyle and my job to make sure I am self-cared for to operate well. I began to tweak things that needed to be let go of and bring in more of what I needed. I prioritized and realized my needs and what was to stay with me, as well as what was depleting me and had to let go of.

It was hard to let go of certain things, such as long term friends, family, and locations that I traveled to, and the lifestyle I used to lead as a Russian Old Believer cultured woman. Transitioning to a new Americanized lifestyle had no restrictions but I knew I had to let go to be what I am to be. If I didn't keep going forward, I would be setting myself backwards in life. I then received a divine message that I needed to be with my own kind of people, and practice my inner work and meditation, but not for long periods of time.

As I detached from what wasn't serving me, this book showed up to be written after a year of solitude and inner realignment, as the book surfaced, I then realized why I had to detach from certain environments and be in my own kind of environment to create, and to have that energy to hear the guidance that was coming in from my spiritual team.

Becoming the Refined Tool

We are all instruments of all kinds. It is important to know your demeanor and how it represents itself to bring out the best in you and what your expertise is. It is important to honor what flows through you, as in your work.

What do you mean by that?

Meaning you must "be" before you create—you must know who you are before you can create. Whether as your vision, your trust in the self, your own value—it can be in any form. At times we are already what we need to be, yet cannot see or understand why we operate as we do. We then begin to discover what we are actually capable of and what we were destined to produce.

Not all need to be high maintenance, but some do. To care is to give and to care where their direction of energy goes. The aware ones protect their energies to such an extent because they know what they need to be and do for themselves and know how valuable it is.

Through you all things can happen.

Ask yourself the following questions:

Do you know what you are for?

If one can know what they are for, one will stand in that place of themselves to a very high degree. We are all equipped and equipped well. When in realization of one's equipment, one can operate well.

What mastery do you have hidden in you that you need to unravel?

Have you truly surrendered to yourself?

What do you harness on a day-to-day basis to refine you as a valuable tool?

What do you need to do to build and to become and to expand?

Suggested "Snob Within" Practice

Fill in the blanks.

I don't like _____ because _____.
It makes me feel _____.

I want instead _____.

I will choose _____ over _____
any day. Why?_____

I value _____ it's why I know I don't value _____
and choose to release _____ by _____.

I find _____ is interfering with my _____
because _____.

Instead of _____, I want _____.

For this, I choose to be more aligned with _____
than _____.

I know I value myself more than _____
because _____.

To rise above it, I will _____ because it will make me feel _____.

My top priorities in my life are

1.
2.
3.
4.
5.

I feed my priorities by focusing daily on

1.
2.
3.
4.
5.

I allow my priorities to grow in my life by

1.
2.
3.
4.
5.

Affirmation: I feel and understand my own high value, and flow through me and into my creations, my productions, and love how naturally it all flows through me.

CHAPTER 13

We Judge

As we judge anything, in the process, we learn more about ourselves on what is our priority and the importance it has in our lives.

I asked the spirit guides: Can judgement actually be a good thing?

Judgment is an interesting approach in life to anything because it takes courage to see and know what is desired and what is not, and to rise into the true essence of the desires. All that one desires usually attracts into their own future through judgement. Many think judging is a negative approach to a way of life and toward anything, although it does bring clarity and through that you learn what you truly desire. The comparison only shows to us what is important to us, and that we desire it in our life as well, or to learn more of who we are in that process of comparison, whether it may be to another person, situation, even things as a lifestyle. It can also be subtle as an achievement or accumulation of some kind. Judgement allows us to see how murky the water is. To judge is to see it truly as it is, and to realize then that we want clear water. We realize with judgement first so as to process what we're seeing and to align ourselves with what we truly desire to have, be, and do in our own life.

Was judgement formulated among humanity or do you think it was given from day one?

It is an awareness. Judgement comes in many forms and can be applied to anything to realize, recognize, and then continue into what is ahead of them to be on the path. This kind of awareness was on this planet not just for humanity but for all to have decision and action from that place.

What is judgement anyway?

Judgement is when one needs to evaluate what is and what is not. When this happens a decision is made, as it is an assessment.

Judgement also may be misused to analyze in a way without realizing their energy is wasted without a final decision. All this is from an awareness of knowing when to judge and what to judge. Some things are judged simply to entertain, yet not to apply to self in any way. This can be a learned approach, although those who are beyond entertainment know and value the energy it takes to give out in order to receive, as this can help with the final decision.

As we walk through gardens of roses and courtyards filled with other humans, our perception sees what we want and what we don't want. Wilted roses, lush roses, fragrant roses, and roses with no scent at all. Healthy humans, not so healthy humans, your kind of humans, not your kind of humans, fortunate humans, and not so fortunate humans. They are all assisting in allowing us to focus on ourselves. They help us realize what we need to focus on within ourselves to improve and attract more of what we desire. Wilted roses may show us we need more water and more nourishment. Looking at the wilted flower, we have the ability to assess our inner self and ask did I have plenty of water to drink today? Do I gain strength from the environment I am in now?

As for being in the courtyard of humans and roses, we may analyse and inner-criticize others not to hurt or to put them down in any way, but only to know what we want for ourselves. Humanity and things around us are powerful tools of personal development and growth and realizing your own desired realized self.

What is self-judgement in the spiritual realm?

Self-judgement in the spiritual realm is omnipresence.

What do you mean by that?

Meaning one will judge the self to reach omnipresence.

Can you explain that?

I am omnipresent. I am present with you. Do know you are not alone. We speak and collaborate together as one consciousness at this moment. You and I are one, as Karen Martushev.

I do understand you want to know more about this subject. Omnipresence is a divinity of the self. A place within the self that one can reach by heart and mind judgements to alter consciousness. Both the mind and the heart need judgment, for judgement creates life. If there is no judgement, there is no creation. To create one needs judgement from a constructive place.

When there is no judgement, a presence occurs. Being fully present with self is called omnipresence, the highest level of presence and engagement with the self.

Judgement will reside in each and every one of us to alter such consciousness. Judgement is a gift given to humanity to alter their consciousness. If one masters the knowledge of judgement, one may use judgment to master the self to evolve a presence in the self, and maintain it through that as well.

If one cultivates judgement well, one may become who they always wished to be and have that presence in them, as an emotional alliance.

Omnipresence disintegrates judgement and destruction in the self. One who can be omnipresent is a bliss to others and to themselves. Destruction may be present in the judgement stage of the self when in the process of reaching the level of omnipresence. Omnipresence is a process one undertakes to evolve and be.

As for a physical human plane, if aware enough, judgement may be seen as a constructive step in order to build one's self and one's life. Judgement builds into desire, and judgement is the mechanism that helps one to get there. Judgement may disintegrate confusion when applied correctly and used to one's need, whether in negative or positive format. One enters judgement to create one's life.

My Human Experience

As my awakening began I felt a sense of heightened awareness and felt I was becoming unstable and not in my physical field. I felt I was losing a lot of my personal development habits that I'd grown over many years. I was awakening spiritually so rapidly that I felt the fragmentation of my physical body and I had to fully depend on my husband for support and not work for a few years. Luckily, the business was doing great and increased in income every year covering his expenses, my expenses, and money set aside for travel and the transition of life.

In those five to six years, my judgment of myself, others, and everything around me was super high. I judged everyone and everything in my sight, including myself. I realized then why at the time I was doing so, but I kept going because there is always light at the end of the tunnel. I felt and began to understand that I was pushed to rise into something, and releasing something yet unknown to me and somehow had the energy to do so, as the past few years were not pretty and quite messy. But today after so many years when I look back I see I was given the time and space to take that step for the transformation to take place, and be committed in the proces, and this includes the day I began my personal self thought journey.

Over the years, especially in the last couple of years, my healing began to show me that judgment is good and I would get these amazing downloads on how judgement is good for the desired direction of evolution and life ahead. After receiving the downloads of the divine consciousness, I began again to get back to business and create programs to offer to the public on activating their own true purpose and aligning with their own inner zen and bliss, especially to moms that are going through what I went through and who want to have a better lifestyle or need more calmness in their homes and within themselves. I also worked with those who wanted a deeper understanding of their own existence here on earth, and how they can assist their family and future generations. I also got a website built by a lovely lady and have a podcast out on iTunes called Being Divine Light. I do know I have been called to create a few more things and I allow them to unfold naturally as they are meant to.

I allowed this to take place in myself and used the judgement for constructive reasons to grow definicity through my desires into fulfilling my universal assignments. During this time I realized that there was a pattern: every time I was expanding or altering my consciousness, negative judgement would show up. So I began to ask why. I started to assess myself as if I was my own client and cultivated my connection with my inner self.

Through this process, I knew my energy was being depleted in the judgment phases, I felt tired, and overheated, I knew something was up in those times. When I worked through my judgment sooner, I felt more balanced, soothed and calm.

Every time now I feel judgement coming over me or a similar emotion, I already know there is expansion going on inside me that I need to assess, realize, and welcome in. I've learned to allow the energy to be directed in a way where it's soothing to me and others around me. By being aware of what causes me to judge and where it is coming from and into what area of my life, then I go into that place of myself and begin my process of being more present in that area, and see what I need, and subconsciously want or desire. Although at times I learned it is also what I did not allow in such as a spiritual gift that was opening up, a mission to fulfill or clearly a divine message of awareness to receive. This is why meditation was given to master and evolve into and use when needed. This was my journey of judgement.

Below I will share my self assessment, which I do from time to time on myself. I know I am only here to share my journey and what helped me to overcome it and to use this practice to the best advantage on what was given in our lives. This practice below is not mandatory, and is not here to heal or prescribe, only to share and self care.

Self-Care Assessment

What do you judge in yourself now? Make a list.

Who and what do you judge in your life? Make a list.

What do you judge in others? Make a list.

After you complete these lists, assess what emotions are playing out in the process of judgement more. What is the emotion that shows up most for each list?

Then to transmute the judgement, for each item you wrote in the lists above, rate on a scale from 1-10 how much energy each judgement statement takes away from you energetically, emotionally, physically, mentally, and time-wise.

This will allow you to see how much presence of yourself is taken away from you to experience in your own life.

The third step is to see how you can shift your activities, your mindset, your focus, your presence or your morning routine to be more present in those areas.

Consider what you wrote down as a list that you judge yourself on. If there is none, skip this step. Now rewrite it in a way that says what you want to experience more of in yourself.

Consider what you wrote down about what you judge in your life. Rewrite it in a way that says what you want to experience more of in your life instead.

Consider what you wrote down about how you judge others. Rewrite it in a way that says what you want to experience more of in your life or self.

Allow your judgments of yourself, your life, and others to guide you toward your needs, your wants, and much more.

What is missing in your life that you want to have, be, do, and experience?

Now ask yourself the following questions:

How can I be more present with what I want to experience in myself?

How can I be more present with what I want to experience in my life?

How can I be more present with what I want to experience with others?

These three powerful questions are a really great exercise to get things going in your life again. It also builds great focus that gives the heart energy and ambition to take action.

#Affirmation: I am my own true knowingness and am aligned with my true desired presence. Through this I experience and receive what I was destined for.

CHAPTER 14

Neglect

Neglect is to deny the highest level of result one could achieve.

I asked the guides: What is the spiritual meaning of neglect?

Neglect in the realm of spirit is quite divine, although it may not suit humanity as it does here. Here neglect means a deep understanding of what one connects to more than other areas. Meaning that we are all categorized in a way where we do not need to be; there are many things a human needs to function on an earthly realm. Although as a human there are more complexities needed to care and to be, as responsibilities on earth are more complex and more dense in a way that we here are not. Our needs here are different from human needs. Human harmony versus spiritual harmony may differ, too, since responsibilities are different.

There are times when one can neglect a certain area of their life without notice then question why it is failing them. But why does neglect happen?

All the neglect that happens is a form of accumulation toward oneself, such as too many distractions and disorder in the physical self rather than having balance between the physical and the spiritual being. When one is directed more toward outside of themselves, they take care of that for that is where the focus is. One then realizes that some part of them feels neglected and doesn't know why. This alone can create disharmony among the physical and inner world of one'sone's existence. When taking the focus from the external world and bringingbringing it back to the inner existenceexistence of oneself, we then can see if we neglect any part of ourselves while fulfillingfulfilling things in our exterior world.

To overcome neglect and similar emotions, one is to face one's needs and identify what needs nourishment. For this I mean choosing a consciousness, and a system to engage with and replenish, and nourish as a living mechanism. For the path to open before you, the direction must be open to harmony.

What is the emotion that creates neglect the most?

Facing something in life without a certain kind of awareness can create neglect, or when going through something in life, as the energy is not there to self care or even move forward. Neglect can also be when one's energy is directed into a certain direction without giving attention to another. A lot of the time when we prioritize what is important to us, and what is needed to take action on, that is the time imbalance and certain kind of neglect shows up, especially those who have very busy schedules, as there are the self replenishing days to balance it out and have harmonious flow in life.

Balance is flowing energy into all areas of life needed without neglecting another—a way of self-studying and tweaking a life and self for them to create balance. The goal is for one to compliment another, as action meets existence.

For this many confuse what being in balance means, yet one may truly never prioritize it or consider what it means to them, or how it is to be experienced. Many can consume information on how to become balanced, yet are left confused as to how to apply it to their own needs.

Balancing a part of life is to give a deep meaning to that part of life. By giving to the self in that area as a giver to the self, one can take full presence in that area of life. That is when balance can take place and realization comes in about how nourishment is needed to flourish. Many may function in only one or two areas of life, that can have a domino effect to other areas of life and balance them out naturally, and that is all that is needed for them to truly live their purpose. However, others may need most areas of life open and balanced to fulfill their purpose.

Those who seek balance in life are seeking harmony. What exists and how we exist may create friction and lead to neglect. When in harmony, this leads to nourishment and improvement by the natural ability of harmony.

How so?

Neglect is a form of lack of focus. When focus is given, one has the power to transmute it by giving it attention. Through attention, we may attract and experience harmony and as we emerge into harmony, there resides our own self in that state of being and presence. So into that presence we go and feel loved and nourished by our own self and our emotions. That can naturally begin the transmutation process into something one desires to grow into.

Subjects of Harmony

Many emotions may reside in harmony. Harmony may take place in anything as a circumstance, connection, expression, thought, or in any other way possible, but when one feels the disconnect of their own harmony from themselves and their true inner world, that is where the energy of friction and neglect begins to come in. At such times, one may be questioning or feelingfeeling emotions that are not harmonious.

In harmony we find good, positive things in life and in there our joy resides. Through that joy, we then feel a sense of accomplishment, a sense of being, and a sense of our own true divine. Although not in all cases harmony may reside in, for there is a more serious, highly developed circumstance where things need to be done in that format for the greatest result. Meaning when things need to be done under pressure we at times need to be out of our own way to complete a task, take action, to receive and such we won't experience harmony, but courage, strength and mission at heart instead. This alone and again depends on what your purpose, desires, and mission is in your life to fulfill as a universal assignment.

Applying Harmony to Action

Inner harmony is something more felt, not as much seen, as at times there can be so much chaos outside ourselves yet we can feel inner harmony and in cases observe and see how two worlds can be so different. Inner harmony is something from within that one cultivates and feels. A feeling of harmony may propel a human into endeavors one can only imagine. As this takes place, especially when unplanned, you will be connected with yourself and to harmony. You may be wondering how to know when one is experiencing harmony. One will be connected to time within themselves. That is to say, when it is time, harmony comes in and action is taken in a divine time frame. Flow is experienced in the process and harmony is the feeder of the flow.

When I was in harmony with myself and the universe, I would know and feel it. By asking what I want and what I need, I would receive it quickly. The times I would ask and wouldn't receive it soon, I learned it wasn't time, or it wasn't for me. This then aligns me to receive in its place what I was meant to. At times I knew I was not in harmony––when I would experience things that I knew were not mine. In those times I would go into solo time and into my meditation and ask the universe for my harmony back. It would come back.

By not asking what we want or need from our higher self or the divine is self-neglect. Many don't realize this because things are hard at times and we can be deeply connected to hardship rather than using our energy to rise above hardship by asking what we need, want, and the guidance with it. For this reason, it's important to practice self-care and know our inner self's needs and wants to keep going as well as the ability to ask and energetically align. Life has a need of inspiration, creativity, movement, expression, and such, and all this needs resources, help, and divine guidance to form.

Below I will share a self care, a self direction practice I hope you enjoy––again it is not mandatory.

Embodying Harmony Worksheet

What areas have you neglected in your life?

What areas of your life do you feel more disconnected from and what times did you notice that you feel disconnected?

What area of your life and or in yourself have you felt more frustration than experiencing your kind of harmony?

If you were to embody more of the harmony within yourself, what would you feed more through that energy in your life? (Choose a goal or a desire.)

As for the last question, what does harmony mean to you? If you actually had it to the extent needed, what would that mean to you? What would shift and change in your life or your perception?

To experience more harmony in your life, what do you need to ask for?

What resources?

1.
2.
3.
4.
5.

Relationships? Connections?

1.
2.
3.
4.
5.

By embodying harmony, what emotions do you want to attract to experience more in your environment and life?

1.
2.
3.
4.
5.

What character or personality traits would you like to acquire or grow into?

1.
2.
3.
4.
5.

Complete the following paragraph: This is a custom affirmation you created for yourself.

I have true harmony in my life now, and I have resources, such as _____. I take time for self care, especially in _____. This creates the energy to create (or have) _____.

After completing the paragraph, read this affirmation out loud to yourself and you will see what nourishment you need for the life, growth, or creation you want to bring forth. Realizing your nourishment needs will also show you the areas of your life that are currently yearning for your undivided attention.

CHAPTER 15

Bliss

It first begins shifting in your mind and heart and then in your own reality.

The receiving is the most profound way of having something with ease and with true intention, and a deep knowingness in this all is able to be. This is the nature of bliss and has great ability to give as well. Here all is divinely open and is flowing and all is truly abundant and nourished. It is a place we all have within us and we all have the ability to enter that place of ourselves. This is the power of bliss that was given to each and everyone of us. Do not deny your own bliss for bliss is you.

As I was writing this book, each chapter was given one at a time without any outline like a usual book would have prior to writing. But when I finished the last chapter thinking that was it and I was finished with the book, this chapter then was quickly given, and I am very excited what they will share with us here. I do know there is great bliss after a deep spiritual awakening and a deep transformation for a higher self to take place in oneself, as I am also learning through this book why such change takes place in one's life.

I asked the guides: What is bliss in the spirit world?

Ecstasy of the self—a place where pain cannot touch. When pain is transmuted into bliss, there is no pain, only the awareness of bliss. Anywhere pain resides, there must also be a need for realization—usually something to be done and completed so that you might again step into bliss.

Bliss is the highest self here for you. Bliss can transmute pain and create new realities to emerge into. Bliss may be the most powerful healing, soothing emotion to human consciousness that can be known and experienced in physical form.

Why?

When one embodies bliss, all falls away, and nothing can stand in the way of bliss, for it then takes its presence in that area and does what it does graciously.

What do you mean by that?

When bliss takes over, all the other emotions fall away and bliss flows through. Bliss transcends all pain through that one emotion. The power of bliss is the most stable emotion one can emerge into—one is unshakable when one does.

How can we step more into bliss?

By transmuting pain into bliss. One can find hardship in doing so because one must realize that the pain is no longer needed. Pain does serve to awaken and then may be released for transmutation into bliss.

Listening to the body and mind usually can bring you into realization by addressing what is triggering the pain, where pain is coming from, and what it speaks. Even an emotion may speak through us without really speaking a word. It is a mechanism that was given to move us from one step to another. By listening to pain, one can get themselves out of pain and into their own bliss. Bliss is an ecstasy to be obtained. Although not all seek to obtain bliss, and may therefore get stuck in pain and become angry with their inner self and with life.

Bliss is an alkalizing emotion and may overcome anger. Although anger does play its part in nature to bring in situations or phases in the path of realization. Anger plays a part in helping us realize what we no longer need to carry and to realize what one wants more of instead of anger. Not all realize this and do not do the work to reach the states of bliss that are possible within them. Great realization can play a part in embodying bliss and may benefit physical life, not just spiritual awareness and divine consciousness outside human existence.

You may apply bliss in any endeavor in your life and bring about great desire. Bliss may activate a sense of the divine self and may be experienced with others in human form. All lies in bliss and is the highest one could reach in themselves as a human consciousness. As bliss arises in the heart, it may also arise in all your endeavors.

To master bliss, one must consciously align with it and have the desire to obtain such emotions of the self. The energy of bliss can be deteriorated by anger and other forces that create negative heat in the body and mind diminishing the alkaline nourishing life and body oils for the evolutionary self and the descension of the self. Although at times distortion may arrive in life to do removal of what is not needed or is to be diminished in order to begin a new phase in life, this can play out in a negative or positive format so new can take place.

Bliss Consciously

When one soothes the heart consciously by drawing in cooling rhythms to breathe, one can breathe in meditation and breathe in bliss consciously, then release.

The alchemy of bliss is what one may yearn to step into all their life. As we become bliss, everything around us becomes bliss. Be the pillar of bliss and consciously grow and cultivate bliss on a day-to-day basis. The ecstasy may be a grounding or ascending kind, though whichever it may be, it will guide you into your own true bliss. However, bliss may vary person to person. Understanding this will take time––you'll need to realize your own kind of bliss. Knowing this will allow you to detach from other people's bliss and step into your own. You'll be able to define bliss on your own terms, as opposed to what the outside world tells you is supposed to bring you bliss. Wish yourself well and be all that you can be for yourself in the phases of discovering your own bliss.

Begin with the self. Begin with what brings bliss into your heart, and what draws it in naturally, whether it's an environment, an activity, self care or thought form––whichever it may be, commit to it, and cultivate bliss through that daily. Begin being more aware of what makes your heart feel bliss. Surround yourself more with that which brings you bliss. Find more ways and bring it into your life.

My Human Experience

I remember the times I would go through so much pain, I had nowhere to turn but myself. As I went inward, I developed a mechanism to feed myself from the inside, not the outside. For the longest time, I would push my external ego away because when I did feed it, pain would come in from outside sources and environments, and would show up as body pains, pain in relationships, and the pain of life change. As a result, I went inward of myself for years and as I would go inward, nothing that pain would enter, just myself. There I felt no pain, no emotional imbalance, just nothing, all was just *is*. In its place, bliss took residence slowly, and more of similar, if not higher, energies and emotions.

This phase of my life was spent more in deep meditations to soothe the soul, and my inner self began to heal. I became stronger and again focused toward life and looked forward to the future. At times pain kept coming back and I would go back to what gave me bliss, which was meditations by a waterfall nearby in summer, and meditations with chakra music, candles, mala beads, and metal sound bowls in winter in my own home. Through the soothed bliss, more calmness came to my inner self and my environment. I was able to get back to my life and take comfort in knowing I would never truly be who I was before the pain began again. Knowing how to take care of the pain and transmute it with the divine guidance and wisdom given gave me strength and power to really do something about it. That was the greatest gift, and a divine force to rise above it.

Environment

One's environment may bring much pain, sorrow, or joy. All can be comprehended through one mind, one soul, one body. As our environment changes, so do we. Because we are all chameleons, we reunite with and become the environment as we are the environment. As we change, the environment around us changes, and as the environment around us changes, we change. One cannot operate without the other. It is an inner and outer game of ourselves we play to stimulate and align ourselves with what we want to desire, be, and experience.

How can one use an environment to ease pain when in a toxic circumstance?

Abuse from the outside can never be controlled as much as one can control the inner world. It may take time to transmute and to distinguish what is your emotion and what is theirs. Not all the emotions we carry are our own pain. We may take on the burden of others to carry, and I question you: Do you have the strength to do so?

Daily rituals such as meditation or visual practices help grow a consciousness over time, and this is what connects you to yourself, your visions, your life. These rituals allow you to know yourself and how you feel toward yourself, and develop a consciousness that can transmute, grow, and dissolve what is truly not yours to carry. In its place your own true consciousness then takes place allowing you to have great awareness of what is yours truly and what is others'. Your intuition heightens and your connection with yourself heightens the awareness, signaling to you as your divine messenger and letting you know when you are being disconnected from your true consciousness and your true inner connection.

When you find the mind mechanism that is suitable for you, it is then you will naturally grow the consciousness you need through the awareness of your own practice of rituals that benefit your mind.

The mind is the environment for your body, as the body attunes and draws in energy. The mind is the carrier of the environment and is a stimulus for the environment to be what is wanted.

Below I am adding a little self-care and activation for bliss practice, feel free to use it when you need to amp up your bliss within.

The Bliss Cultivation Practice

You might want to use your journal for this.

Ask yourself the following questions:

What can you practice today to cultivate your own bliss?

What brings you pain today? Make a list.

Now rewrite the pain into the positive. Instead of pain, write as bliss instead. See how things can shift for you there.

Example: I experience pain in my relationships because _____. Instead I am experiencing more _____. (Write a whole paragraph on what you want more of that will bring bliss.)

What can you do from your current place to begin cultivating this reality? If you're having trouble thinking of what you can do, try the following:

- Visual intentional meditation
- Journaling on bliss, appreciation, and gratitude
- Using affirmation methods to attract reality in
- EFT tapping

When you commit to any of these, stay on this ritual for a week and see what shifts you feel in yourself, as well as what presents outside of you to match it. Take notes before and after to see if any of these work and, if so, stick with them as your self care system.

Affirmation: I am the center of my own bliss. I experience it everywhere, always, for I am it.

CHAPTER 16
Self-Rebirth

We can self rise and see the birth of the new and the arised one in the self; the new life after death.

In the self is darkness, as one would be in a womb. You may ask, as I did, why some go through the dark night of the soul, and feel this way. One can at times feel as if they are in a womb in that transition to enter a new life. Some will descend as divine masters and ascended masters of the place of is-ness to be here and share wisdom. The reawakened part of the next part of life feels as though it is not yourself, and in these moments things can have a deeper meaning, deeper existence and a deeper creation. As one works and lives from the core of is-ness, not just existence, using the vessel of human existence to express and do what you came here to do: to create things that are a mission, not a want or need, from the place of is-ness.

The self is everywhere for it has no time or dimension. The Is is the self: a mechanism where one goes to feel, wonder, and receive information. The self is beyond the intention, beyond an existence, where all lies and you are there and you are here, and you are everywhere. And you will feel everywhere, for the self is now fully birthed and is flowing through you as the Is, it will always be the Is, and beyond that is nothing else—it is in the core all, and all are one.

The self is the core of all existence and lies in everyone as a network of self. We are all tied into it and it feeds as one big consciousness. We are all parts of it, as the self births in one, all is awakened, all is heard, and all is felt, for the self is in all, and you become all in one human vessel. This is why at times one does something across the world and you feel it within you.

The spirit guides asked me to write this chapter before I ended the book, and doing so made me realize why one goes through such extreme spiritual awakenings in life. In this chapter they gave the reason and I found it very interesting and quite unusual.

As I spoke before, one can create the self and shift from self to self as growth takes place, as Karen did in this lifetime. This takes great mastery and dedication to the self to grow, practice, and be. This is why she was asked to create the course, Evolution of Self, which is not yet created. This divine knowledge was granted for her to share and create to help others.

This course is not made yet, but I was surprised myself when it was given just now, so I guess I now have something to ponder on how it will go about to be fruit here on earth.

You have awakened in yourself the higher self that was with you all along. In it, there are two of you. This does not always occur in your time here on earth, but you from now on will always feel this presence and unite with it as a companion, a wisdom seeker, and a deep divine guide.

When you arise from oneself into a new higher self, one identity becomes two. The soul in this lifetime became two because in the second lifetime there will be two existences of you rather than one. One formats you, Karen, as a female, the other you will see as a man and create family lineage with as man. This is why sexuality suffered for so long in you, as there was not much desire for it or deep human fulfilled desire in that area. In its place was creativity, crafts, such as oil painting, creating beautiful spaces, doing personal development, and having great intuitive visions on steps in life and how to create anything in its place. It seems the sexual energy was more used in a format of creativity until it was truly time in one way or another, and was given as an energy to tap into and use as a life force.

In the journey of awakening, the message from your higher self revealed that you are birthing yourself. What you have created and birthed for the next life is self mastery. Be prepared, that is all.

Experience and the evolutionary completion of the self reaching the evolution needed to split that part of the soul and take it back to where it can incarnate as human. It can carry the same kind of energy as the second one that birthed it, now the two have and can give more of that energy that the planet needs to heal itself, and this kind of evolution Karen does carry and develop naturally through her gifts. Not always, and not to everyone, the soul splits. When it does, great pain occurs and suffering arises in the birthing part of the self. The birthing alone will cause suffering before the soul splits to go into the dimension it is destined to. After the birth, the original stays in human form to serve as a soul mission for the rest of the remaining life, to help to raise consciousness here on earth.

What is the purpose of this self-birth?

When one descends as Karen did on the mission to alter and expand consciousness. This is why rebirth, self-birth, the re-creation of her existence and awareness attunes to very high dimensions. One must hear the self and be guided from above and from all directions, not as a fragment or a part, but a whole being of self, similar to a spirit guide but on a higher level. Many think it's duality, when it's not—in this lifetime she will have this presence with her. The next time she will feel as one when she reunites back with the mother of her consciousness, where all of her self will go after completion here on earth as a human life. Afterwards, she will reunite as one divine form in god's land—that can be as a guide in this lifetime, although it is the infinite part of our self, the part that never dies.

At times she will see herself as a mirror seeing herself, rather than being fully herself here on earth, as the self is also her. When there is disconnection from her own true self, the true source, and from her role here on earth, it may cause the feeling of loss and instability in life here on earth after completing this lifetime.

When rebirth of self takes place one usually is heightened in awareness in the two worlds. She can and does feel that part of her comes in and out and is in other places, while being here as well, and not just in one physical plane. This is new to her and she is still learning this new aspect of being.

This is how she gets information from beyond, and receives it as well.

In that process of descension, Karen found deep pains and dark emotions are only a birth one gives to oneself, and emerges into to become both spirit and physical body. As she descended after reaching the consciousness of the nothingness, nothing in the earthly realm felt normal or comforting. She yearned to go back to that nothingness and took time to truly emerge into these meditations daily, where no pain existed or was felt. All was well there.

To rebirth herself, or one would say renew, she wondered what is to become. Where do people of her kind belong? Why are these physical realms not as divine as the others? Her awareness grew and she longed *for solitude, nature, waterfalls, and oceans. Nature itself has a divine consciousness, which is why it is healing to be in and near.*

As time passed, she realized she can't be in such spiritual meditation bliss always because there were things to do, things that needed her attention, and things she didn't want to deal with. Yet a deep knowingness knew it was time to emerge back into human consciousness and exist in that place on earth again.

It took her years to get back, and today she still doesn't meditate as much because it takes her to high realms in the spirit world.

She learned that even when she doesn't meditate, she can do her mind-emotions processing in other forms, such as a good movie, a workout, oil painting, sewing beautiful custom clothes for herself, and doing metaphysical work in her business. She came into this earth with many gifts and she activated several more once she was here. Still more will emerge in this life. The spiritual gifts activated more after age 33, such as spiritual channeling, conversing with the spirit world, practicing clairvoyance, and tapping into her psychic abilities and more. This is where she is today, blending spirit work with the Law of Attraction and personal development to balance out the spiritual and physical, and offering her services to those who are on a similar path.

The next stage of birth and what happens next will be the emergence of the self. That will be the first step as the soul reunites with the self, and as they become unified that's when they are anchored. Then the self birth emerges to be human, to produce, to create, to lead and do whatever the soul was called here on earth to do.

It may be strange for some to hear this, but in Karen's experience, she has experienced the soul alone and the self alone. As the self and the soul emerged as one in the physical human vessel she walks in today, she knows it is quite strange.

So which one is Karen? She is the soul emerging with her higher self, which is the self. Although she may be both at once, and at times she is only the self walking the planes outside the earthly realms, in the soul she may do work as a human there.

When the soul and the self emerge in a human body, it is rare. But was called for her to be so. This will be what she was called for here on earth.

Many may think this is absurd, but I and many others where we come from have been on the same path.

The creation we come from is not common, although it exists. Where Karen comes from, the soul human part, is from other planes than where we come from, while the self of her is from where we come from. The self has descended into her to let her know we are always with her as family and home, and all the help she needs usually comes from this plane. It was meant for her to awaken to such an extent to where she can hear us.

We are descendants of astrological bodies called liath, where the rare breeds lie. This is why at times Karen feels pains in lower realms and ecstasy in higher realms at the same time. The activation of the self and the soul are in emergence when she feels pain in the lower self and ecstasy in the higher self. Once this is reunited fully, the work will be conducted as one consciousness. The rebirth of the self and the birth of the self will become one.

The soul usually leads in the human planes, as the self is guidance and usually guides the soul to the work one is meant to do.

When one is not full of their own self, their own soul, energies would intrude or live through that space as an intrusion and conduct their own works, their unfinished business. Being the soul-self presence in your own body can help with being stable and connected to your true self, the self that nourishes you back and mothers you. This gives the ability to experience the authentic self, the existence as the root among the self, the one beyond the spirit and the soul that resides in lower chakras to conduct the human work and be seen in the physical world. When this part is being blocked or intruded upon is when the human usually suffers the most. To restabilize one must know their nature, their pain that is physical, not just spiritual and where it is coming from and why. The pain awakens, the physical stabilizes and the relationships propel one in life, once fully present in the part of themselves.

The spiritual awakening and blending with other relationships that were not destined for Karen to be around caused pain and setbacks in life more than ever due to karma from past lives, and those who did not wish well. This was the time she learned to be very strong and very wise, and study herself and know herself and the people she belongs with. She also learned her mission will be mostly solo, for that is how her mechanism operates.

> Rebirth in one life can shift to another to finish what the soul came here to do. Now the rebirth has been completed and Karen is on her way to her own human consciousness. There will also be a new path of life and a new destination. As one rebirths, all may change in a person since inner worlds and outer worlds come together as if born in another body. All things will not be as before the birth and other gifts will come in over time. Many things then change in life as life will not match the old version before the rebirth. Now there is light in the body that did not occur before the birth. For example, coming into the spirit world and coming

> back again is one of the gifts now with Karen to share the light and healing. — Archangel Raguel

You're probably wondering what's next. As you are well on your way and things are unfolding, allow yourself to open in your eye above, for your destiny lies there. — spirit guides

The journey continues...

Look for my next book *The Consciousness Of Self* available soon.